ORGAN

Country Classics

ISBN 0-634-06967-5

HAL•LEONARD®
CORPORATION
7777 W. BLUEMOUND RD. P.O. BOX 13819 MILWAUKEE, WI 53213

Visit Hal Leonard Online at
www.halleonard.com

Any Time

Electronic Organs
Upper: Flutes (or Tibias) 16', 8', 5⅓', 4'
      Add Percuss
Lower: Melodia 8', String 4'
Pedal: String Bass
Vib./Trem.: On, Fast

Tonebar Organs
Upper: 40 7402 001
Lower: (00) 7603 000
Pedal: String Bass
Vib./Trem.: On, Fast

Words and Music by
Herbert Happy Lawson

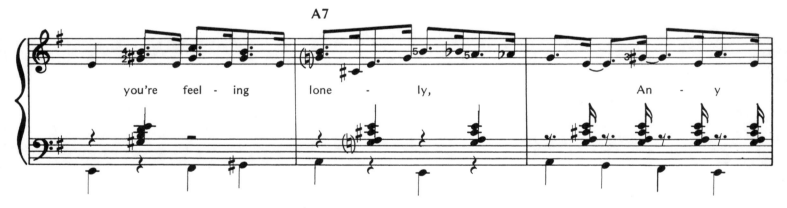

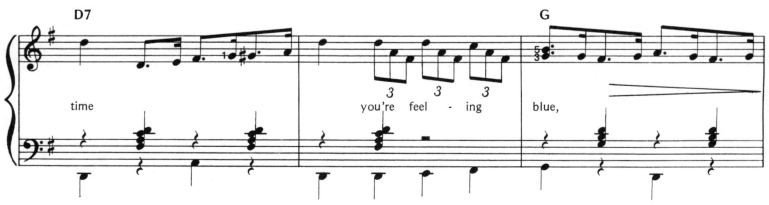

3

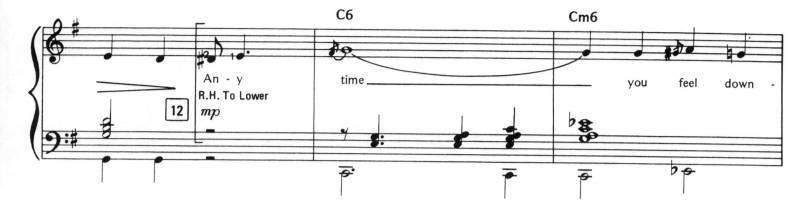

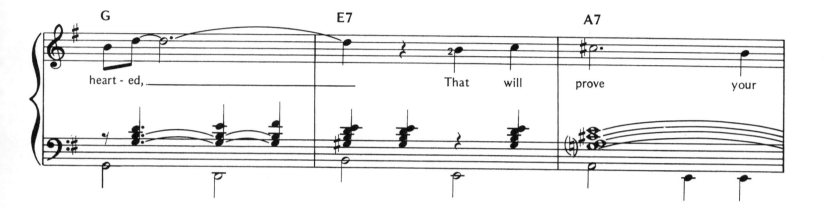

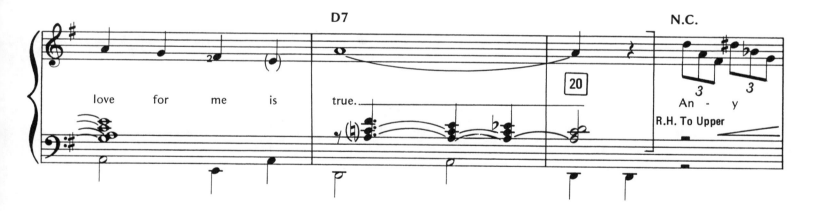

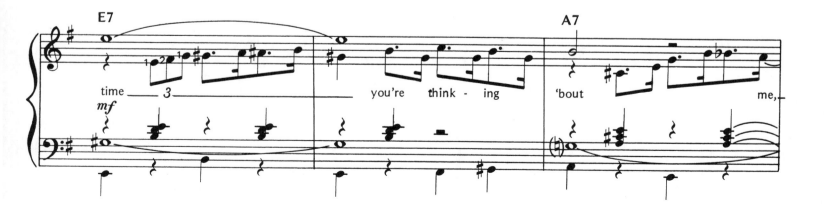

4

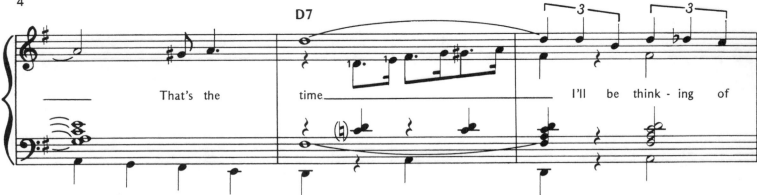

D7

That's the time_____ I'll be think-ing of

B7   E7

you,_____ So an - y time   you

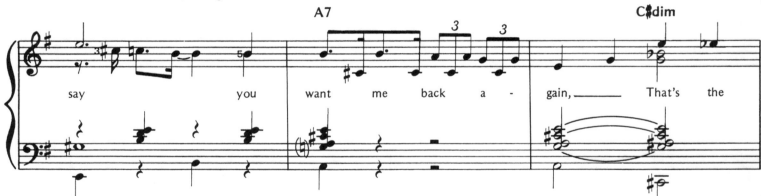

A7   C#dim

say   you   want me back a - gain,_____ That's the

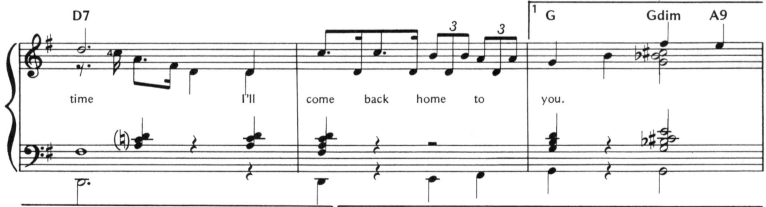

D7   1. G   Gdim   A9

time   I'll   come back home to   you.

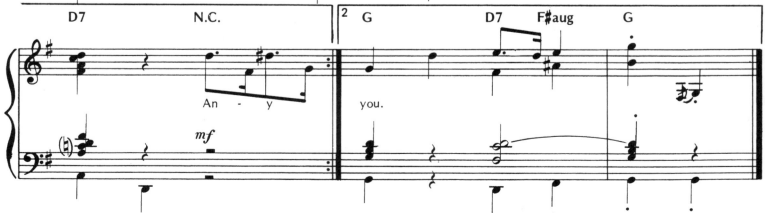

D7   N.C.   2. G   D7 F#aug G

An - y   you.

Crying in the Chapel

Electronic Organs
Upper: Flutes (or Tibias) 8', 2'
       Diapason 8', 4'
Lower: Flute 8', Diapason 8'
Pedal: 16', 8'
Vib./Trem.: Off

Tonebar Organs
Upper: 00 5757 223
Lower: (00) 5523 111
Pedal: 53
Vib./Trem.: Off

Words and Music by
Artie Glenn

With expression

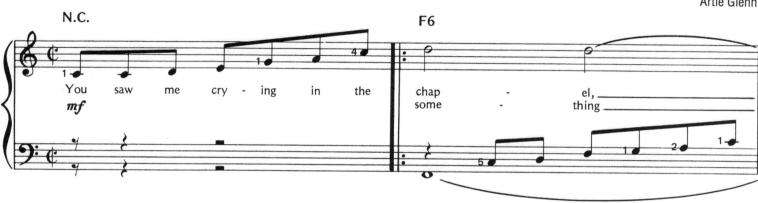

Just a plain and sim - ple chap - el,_____ Where hum - ble peo - ple go to
Meet your neigh - bor in the chap - el,_____ Join with him in tears of

pray;_____ I pray the Lord that I'll grow strong - er,
joy;_____ You'll know the mean - ing of con - tent - ment,

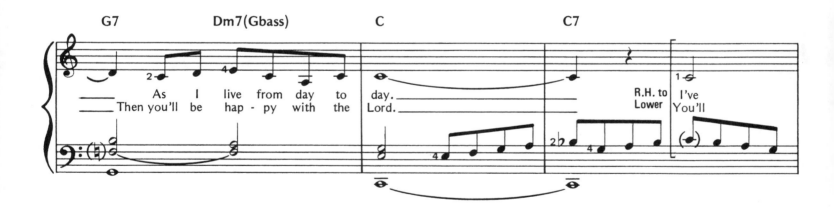

As I live from day to day._____ I've
Then you'll be hap - py with the Lord._____ You'll

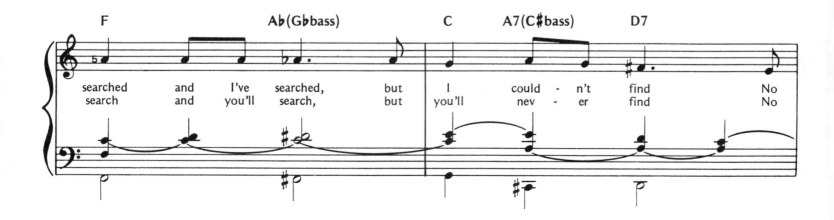

searched and I've searched, but I could - n't find No
search and you'll search, but you'll nev - er find No

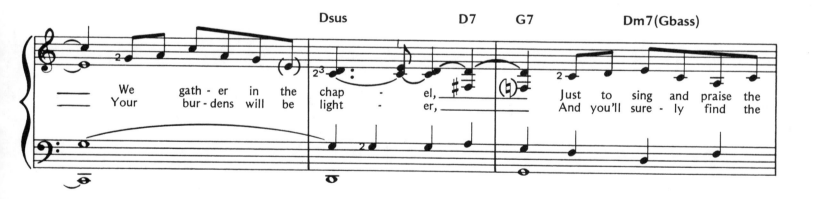

Born to Lose

Electronic Organs
Upper: Flutes (or Tibias) 16', 4'
        String 8'
Lower: Flutes 8', 4', Diapason
Pedal: String Bass
Vib./Trem.: On, Fast

Tonebar Organs
Upper: 80 6616 113
Lower: (00) 7634 212
Pedal: String Bass
Vib./Trem.: On, Fast

Words and Music by
Ted Daffan

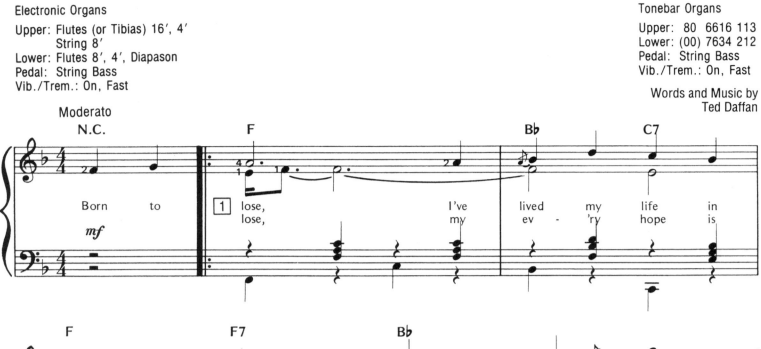

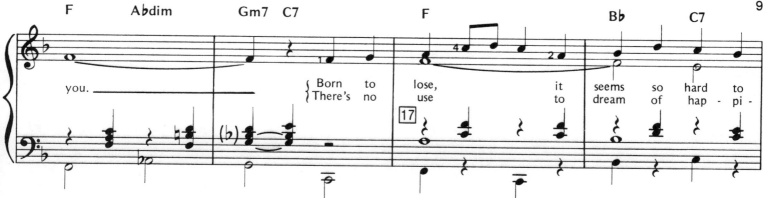

you. _____ | Born to lose, it seems so hard to
There's no use to dream of hap - pi -

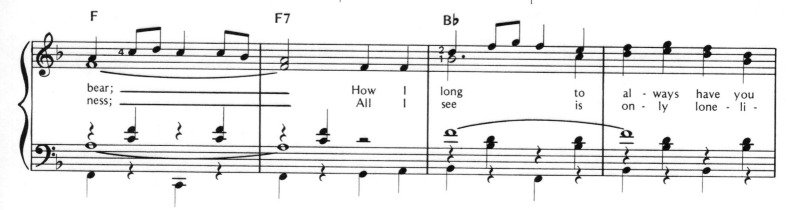

bear; _____ How I long to al - ways have you
ness; _____ All I see is on - ly lone - li -

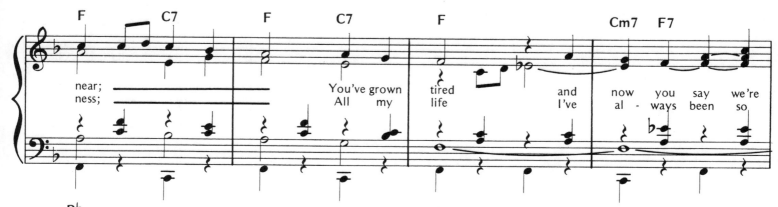

near; _____ You've grown tired and now you say we're
ness; _____ All my life and I've al - ways been so

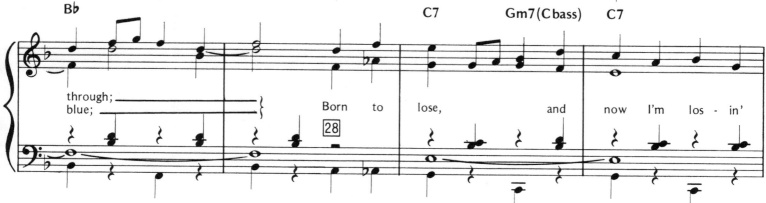

through; _____ | Born to lose, and now I'm los - in'
blue; _____

you. _____ Born to you. ritard.

Candy Kisses

Electronic Organs
Upper: Flutes (or Tibias) 16', 8', 4'
Lower: Reed 8', Flute 4'
Pedal: 16', 8'
Vib./Trem.: On, Fast

Tonebar Organs
Upper: 40 7312 000
Lower: (00) 5402 001
Pedal: 25
Vib./Trem.: On, Fast

Words and Music by
George Morgan

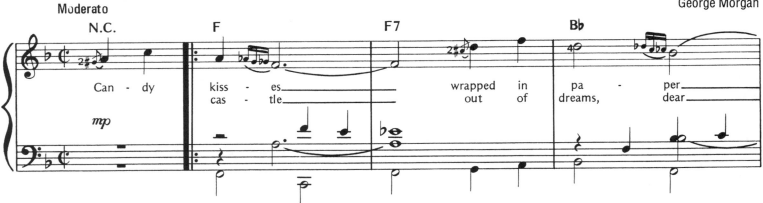

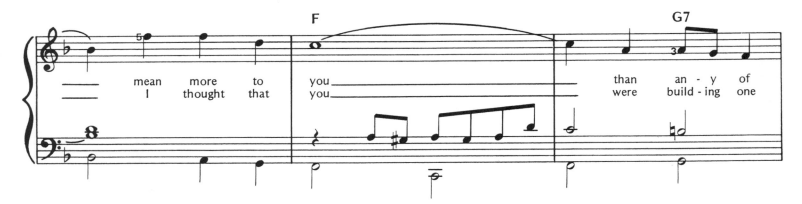

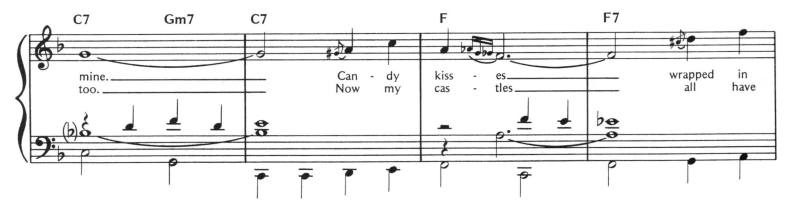

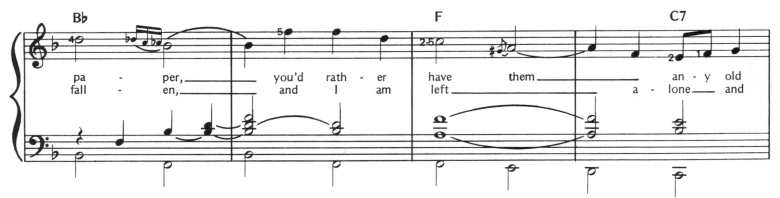

11

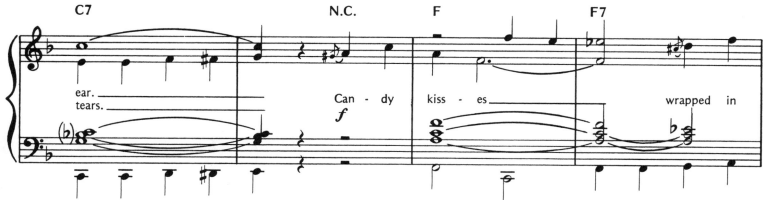

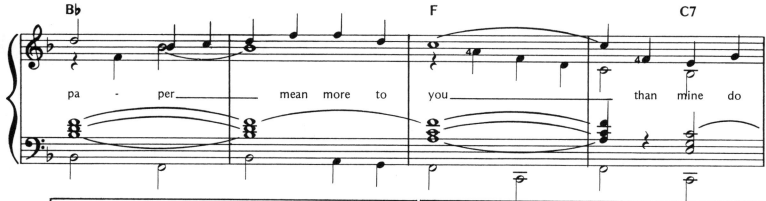

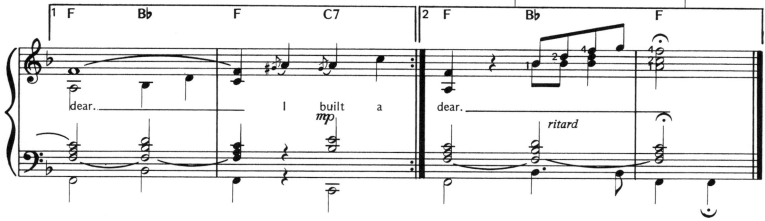

Crazy

Electronic Organs

Upper: Flutes (or Tibias) 16′, 8′, 4′,
　　　Trumpet, Oboe
Lower: Flutes 8′, 4′,
　　　String 8′, Reed 8′
Pedal: 16′, 8′
Vib./Trem.: On, Fast

Tonebar Organs

Upper: 80 7766 008
Lower: (00) 8076 000
Pedal: 36
Vib./Trem.: On, Fast

Words and Music by
Willie Nelson

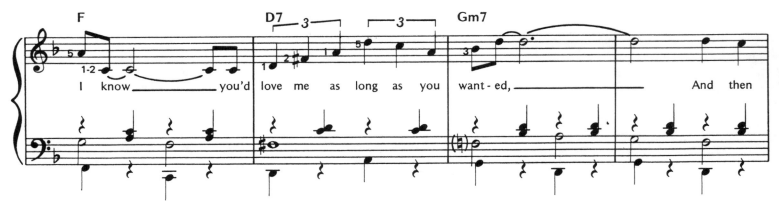

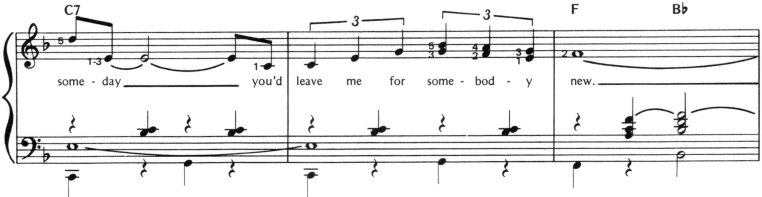

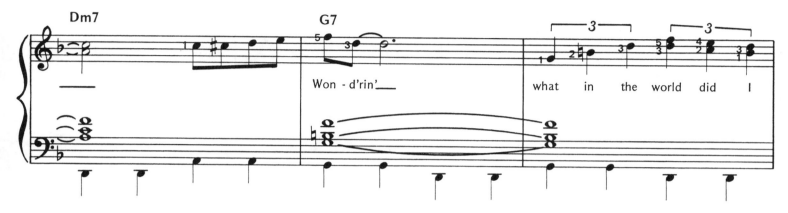

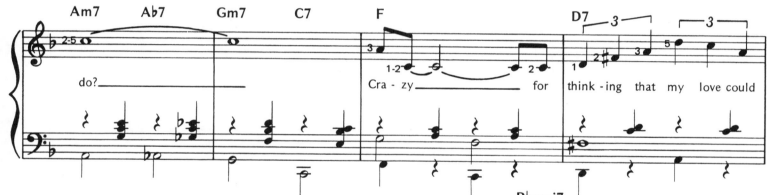

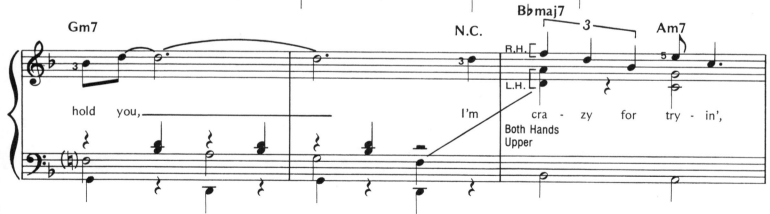

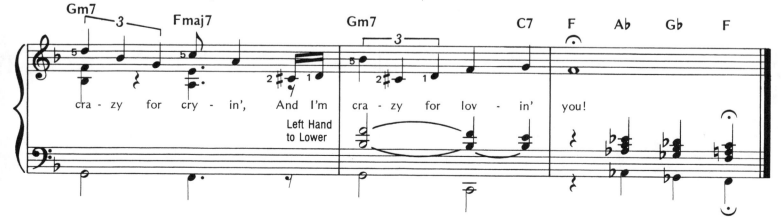

Deep in the Heart of Texas

Electronic Organs
Upper: Flutes (or Tibias) 16′, 8′, 5⅓′, 4′
        Add Percuss
Lower: Flutes 8′, 4′
Pedal: String Bass
Vib./Trem.: Off

Tonebar Organs
Upper: 83 6030 400
Lower: (00) 6402 003
Pedal: String Bass
Vib./Trem.: Off

Words by June Hershey
Music by Don Swander

Brightly

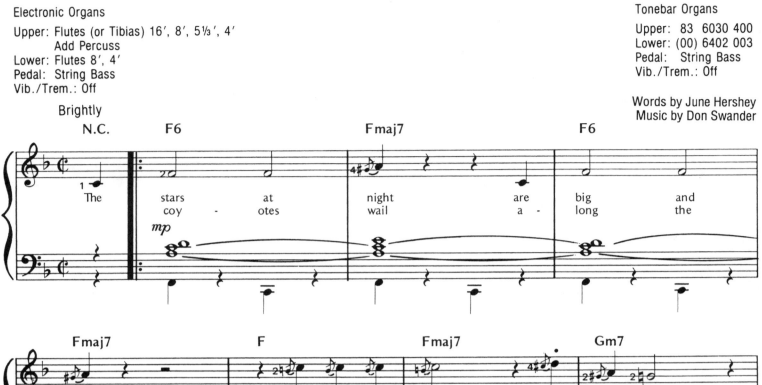

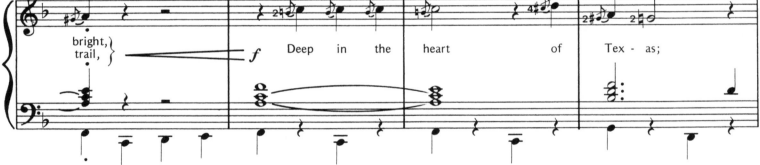

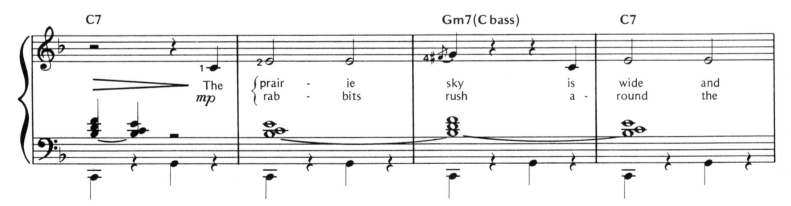

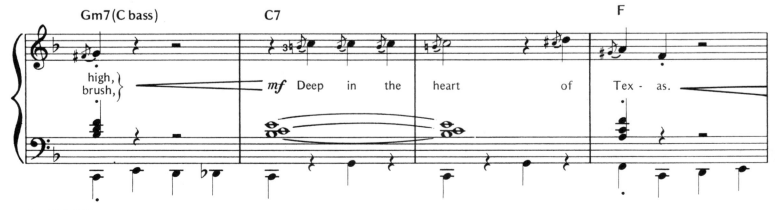

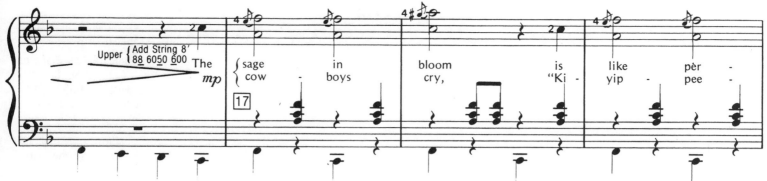

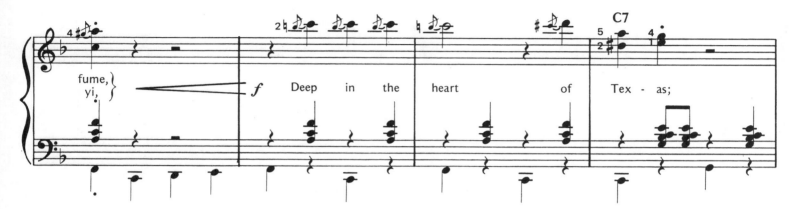

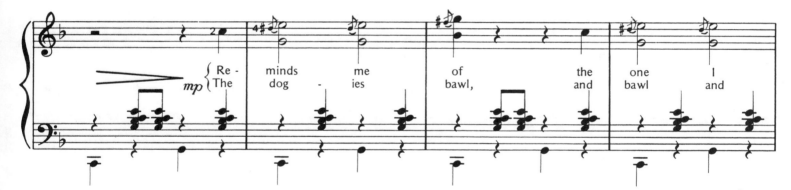

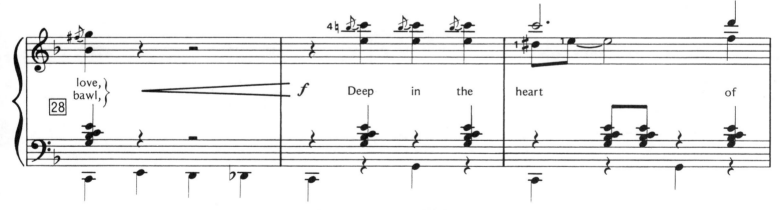

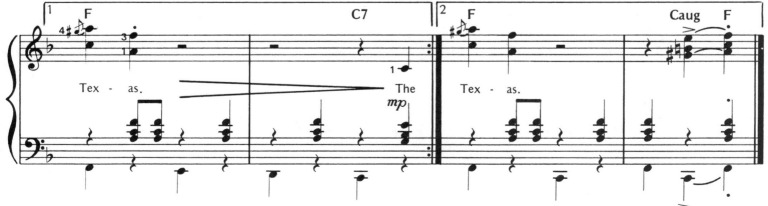

Detour

Electronic Organs

Upper: Preset Piano
Lower: Flute 8', Diapason 8'
Pedal: String Bass
Vib./Trem.: Off

Tonebar Organs

Upper: Preset Piano or
      76 5616 111
Lower: (00) 5523 111
Pedal: String Bass
Vib./Trem.: Off

Words and Music by
Paul Westmoreland

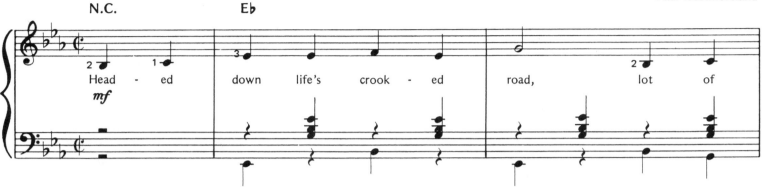

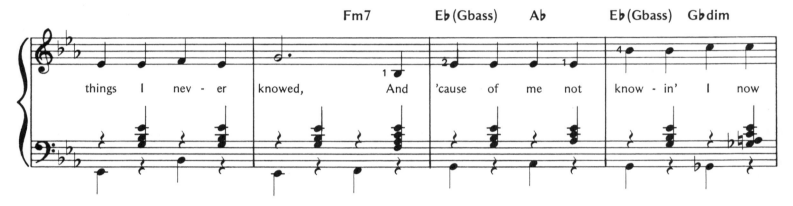

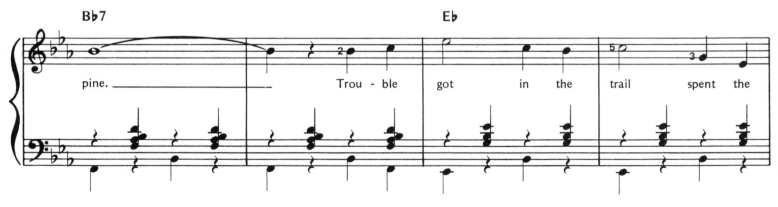

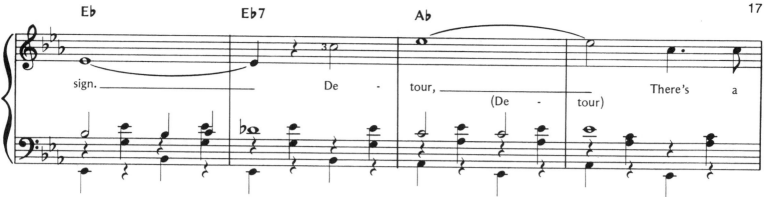

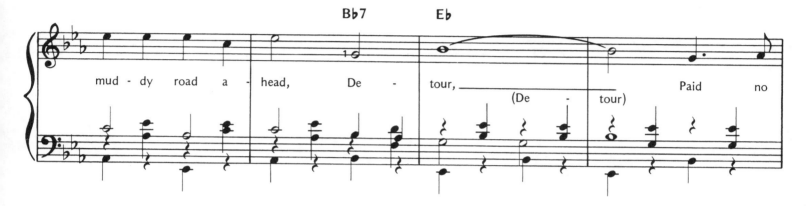

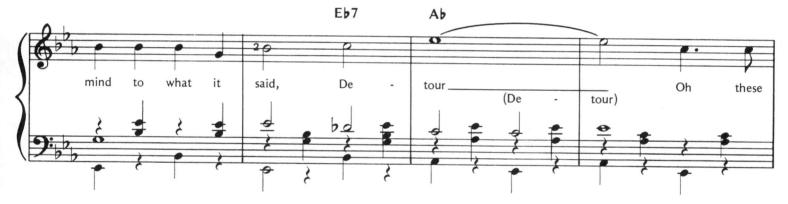

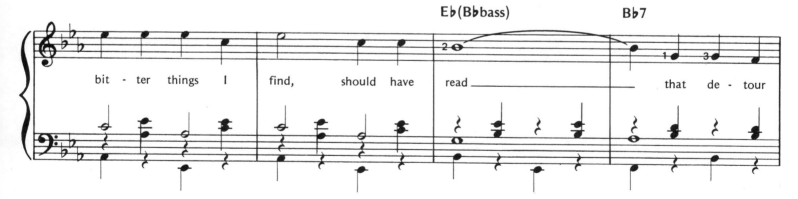

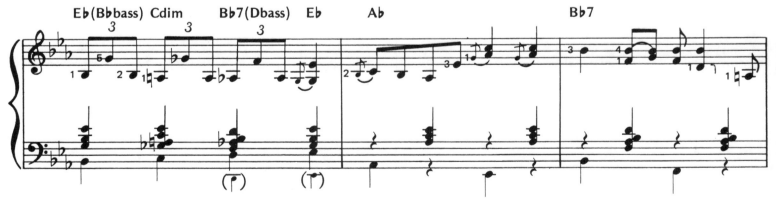

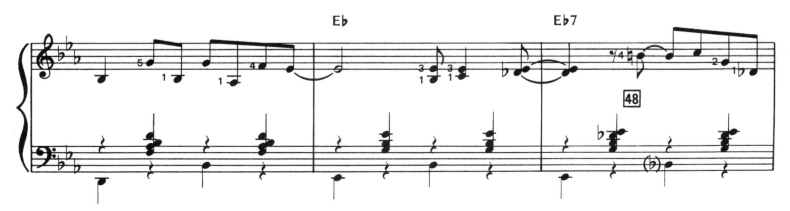

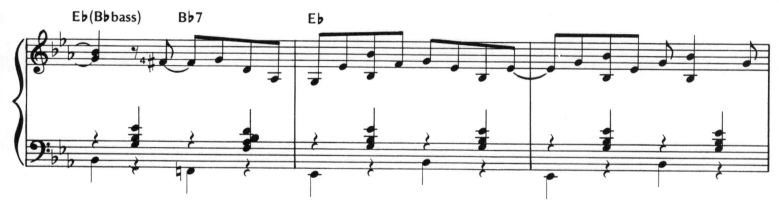

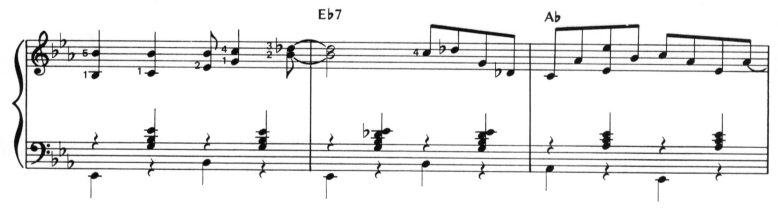

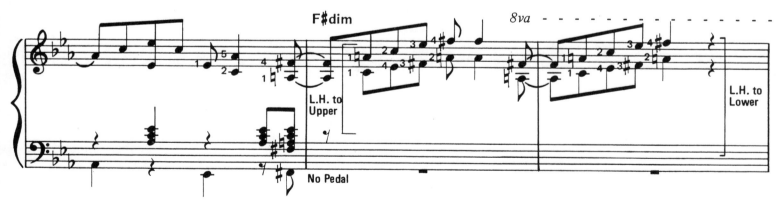

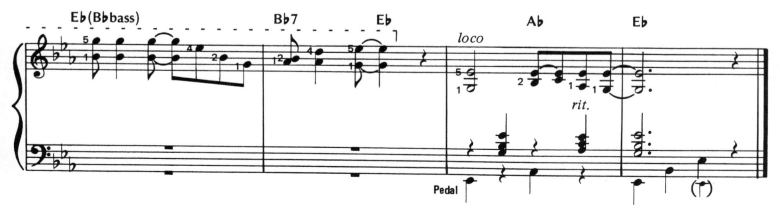

Faded Love

Electronic Organs
Upper: Flutes (or Tibias) 16′, 8′, 2′
        Diapason 8′
Lower: Flutes 8′, 4′, Diapason 8′
Pedal: 16′, 8′
Vib./Trem.: On, Slow

Tonebar Organs
Upper: 84 2354 757
Lower: (00) 8675 007
Pedal: 55
Vib./Trem.: On, Slow

Words and Music by Bob Wills
and Johnny Wills

Vigorously

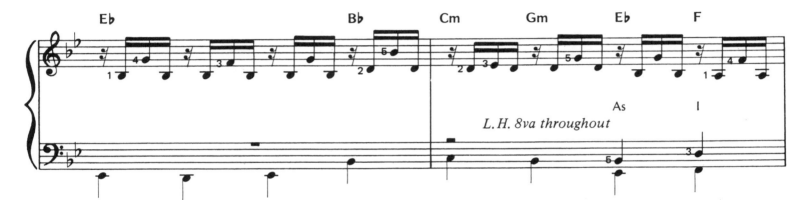

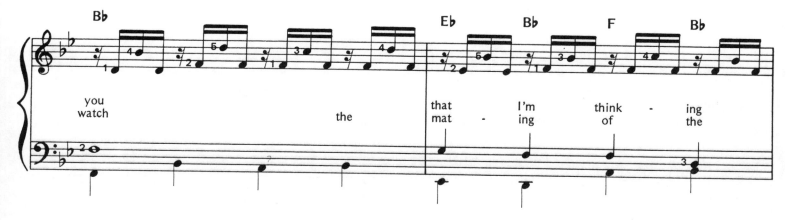

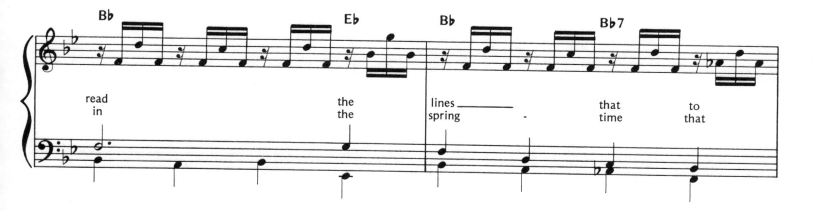

mem - ber our fad - ed
mem - ber our fad - ed

love, _____
love, _____

Fine

Both Hands Upper
loco

No Pedal

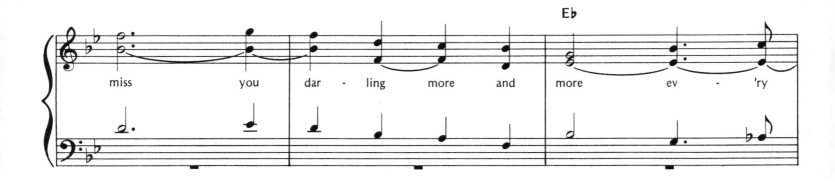

miss you dar - ling more and more ev - 'ry

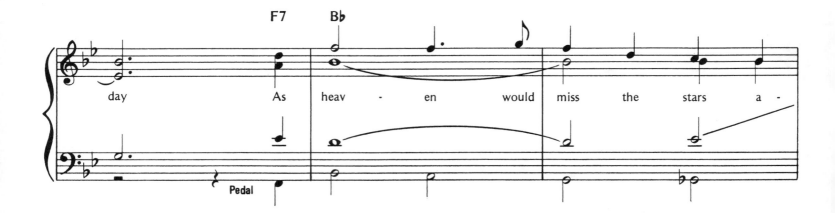

day As heav - en would miss the stars a -

Pedal

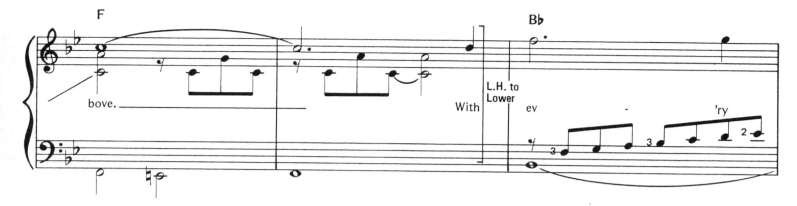

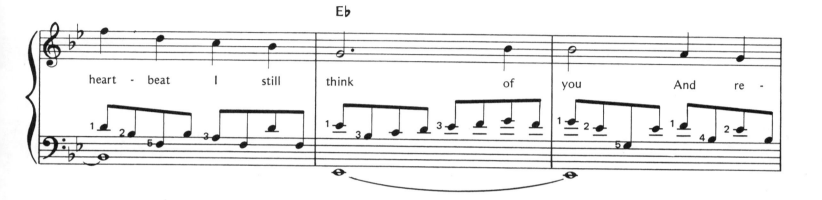

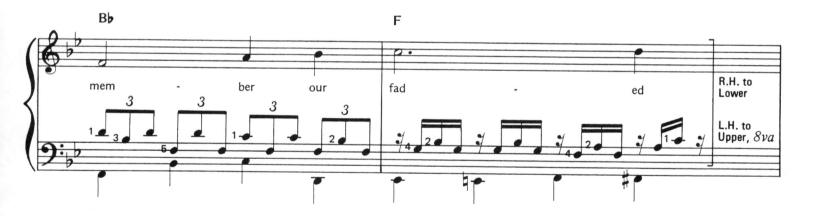

Folsom Prison Blues

Electronic Organs
Upper: Flutes (or Tibias) 16', 4'
       String 8'
Lower: Flutes 8', 4', Diapason 8'
Pedal: String Bass
Vib./Trem.: On, Fast

Tonebar Organs
Upper: 60 3616 113
Lower: (00) 7634 212
Pedal: String Bass
Vib./Trem.: On, Fast

Words and Music by
John R. Cash

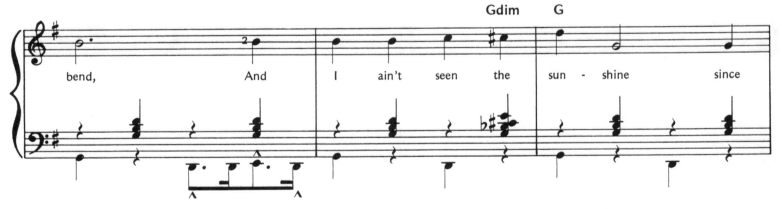

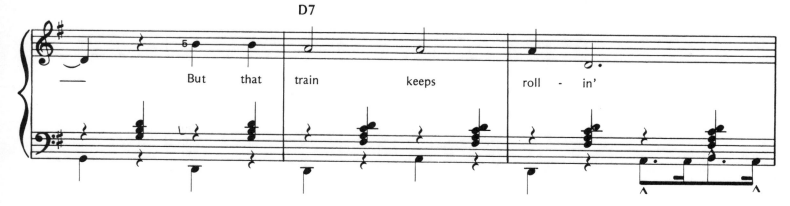

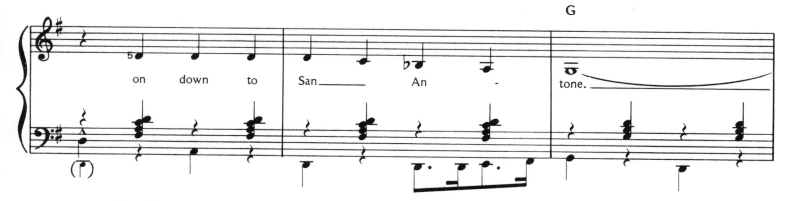

good boy; don't ev - er play with guns." But I

shot a man in Re - no_____ just_____ to_____

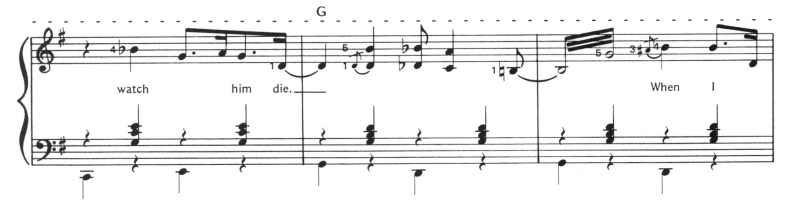

watch him die._____ When I

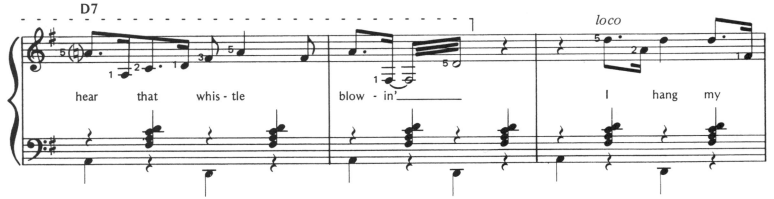

hear that whis - tle blow - in'_____ I hang my

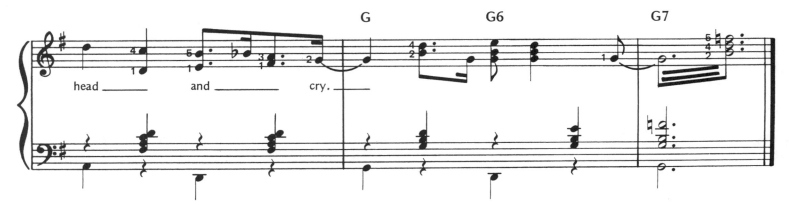

head _____ and _____ cry. _____

Green Green Grass of Home

Electronic Organs
Upper: Flutes (or Tibias) 16′, 8′, 4′, 2′,
       String 8′, Clarinet
Lower: Flutes 8′, 4′
Pedal: 16′, 8′
Vib./Trem.: On, Slow

Tonebar Organs
Upper: 80 8104 103
Lower: (00) 6303 004
Pedal: 25
Vib./Trem.: On, Slow

Words and Music by
Curly Putman

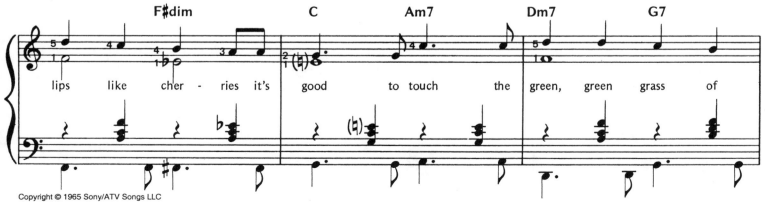

28

home. _____ Yes, they'll all come to

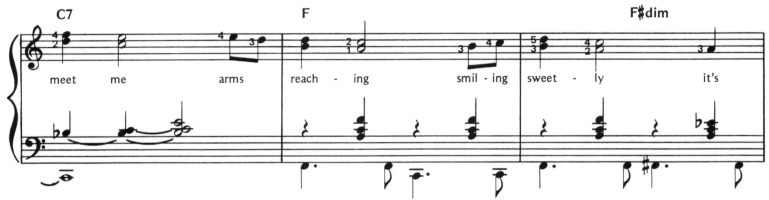

meet me arms reach - ing smil - ing sweet - ly it's

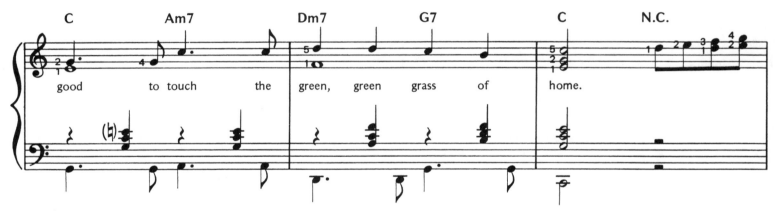

good to touch the green, green grass of home.

The old house is still stand - ing Tho' the

paint is cracked and dry, _____ and there's that old oak tree that

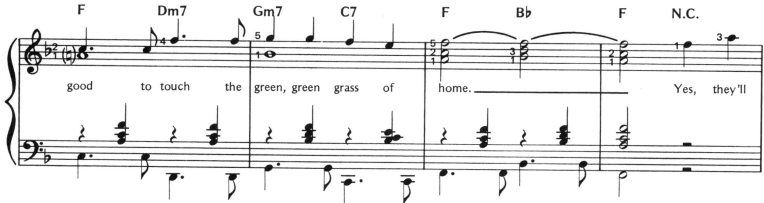

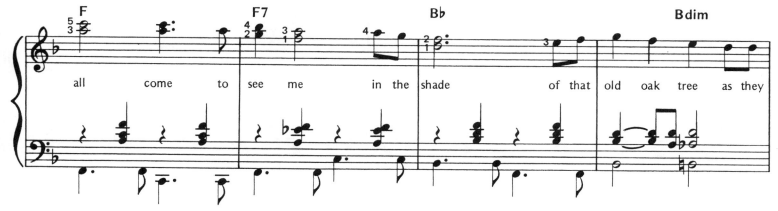

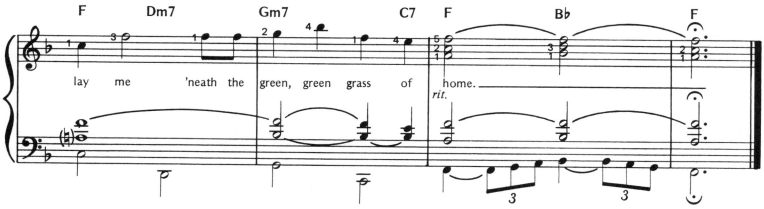

Funny How Time Slips Away

Electronic Organs
Upper: Flutes (or Tibias) 16', 8', 4', 2',
       String 8', 4'
Lower: Flutes 8', 4',
       Strings 8', 4'
Pedal: 16', 8'
Vib./Trem.: On, Fast

Tonebar Organs
Upper: 82 5325 004
Lower: (00) 7345 312
Pedal: 44
Vib./Trem.: On, Fast

Words and Music by
Willie Nelson

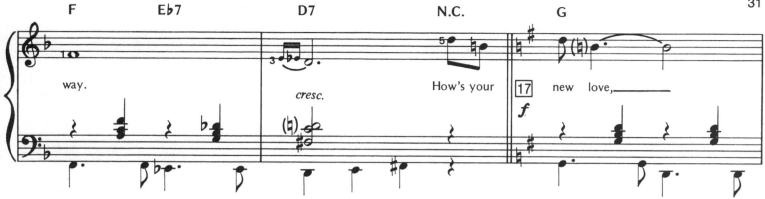

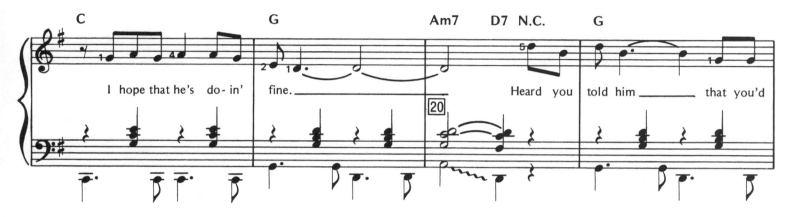

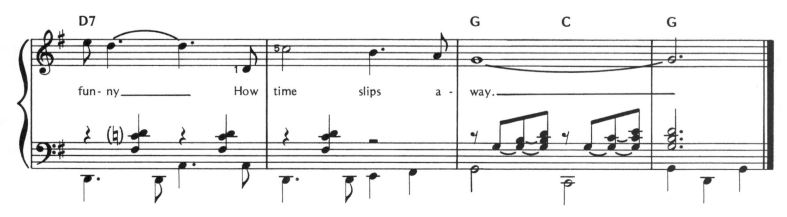

Harper Valley P.T.A.

Electronic Organs
Upper: Clarinet, Strings 8', 4'
Lower: Horn 8, Reed 8'
Pedal: Bass Guitar
Vib./Trem.: On, Fast

Tonebar Organs
Upper: 73 5012 031
Lower: (00) 6304 001
Pedal: Bass Guitar
Vib./Trem.: On, Fast

Words and Music by
Tom T. Hall

34

like to ad-dress this meet-ing of the Har-per Val-ley P. T. A." Well there's

Bob-by Tay-lor sit-tin' there and sev-en times he's asked me for a date Mis-sus

Tay-lor sure seems to use a lot of ice when ev-er he's a-way. And

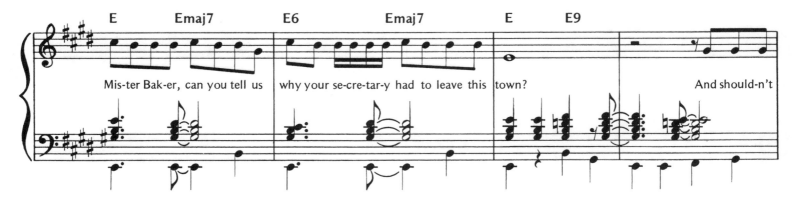

Mis-ter Bak-er, can you tell us why your se-cre-tar-y had to leave this town? And should-n't

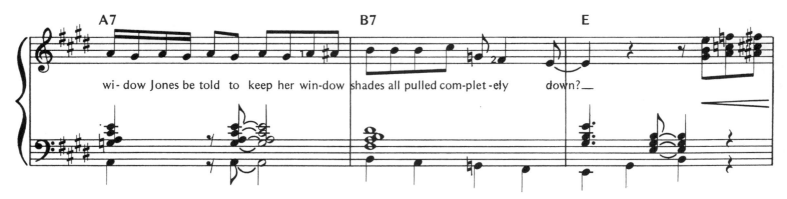

wi-dow Jones be told to keep her win-dow shades all pulled com-plet-e-ly down?

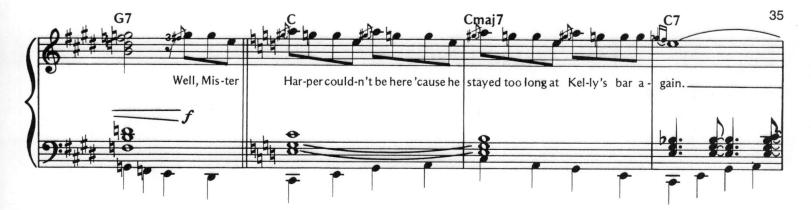

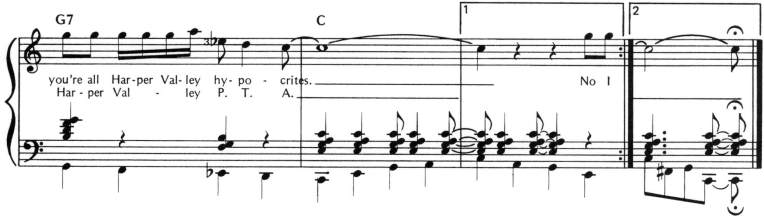

Heartaches by the Number

Electronic Organs
Upper: Flutes (or Tibias) 16', 8', 4'
      Strings 8', 4'
Lower: Flute 8', Strings 8', 4'
Pedal: 16', 8'
Vib./Trem.: On, Fast

Tonebar Organs
Upper: 80 6602 030
Lower: (00) 6534 000
Pedal: 35
Vib./Trem.: On, Fast

Words and Music by
Harlan Howard

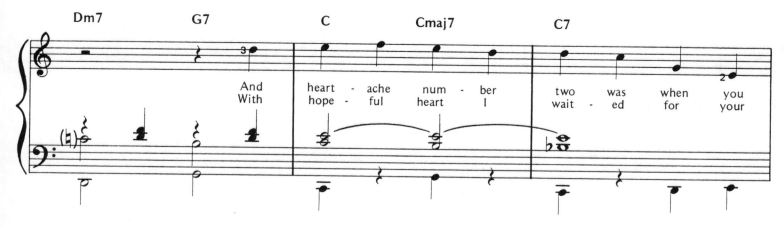

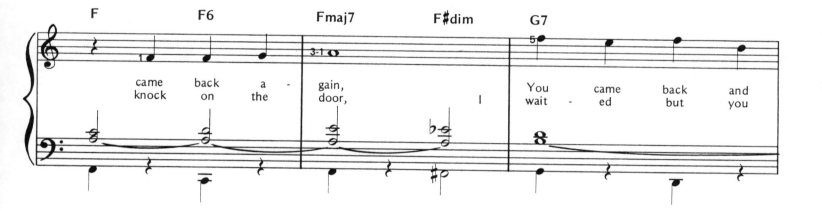

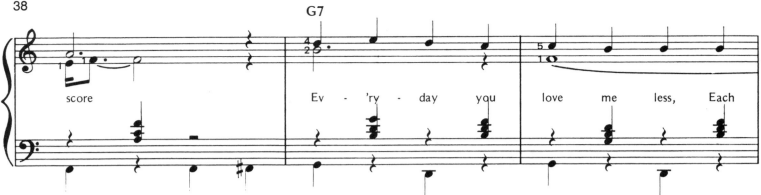

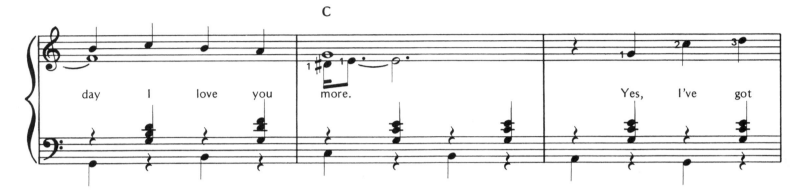

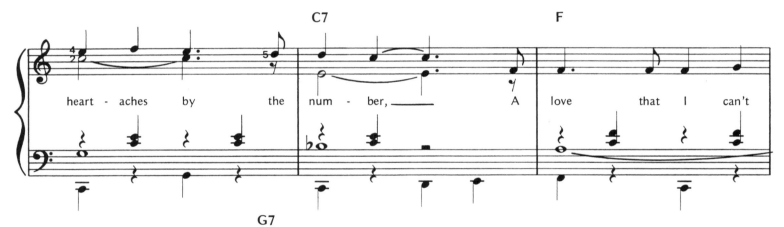

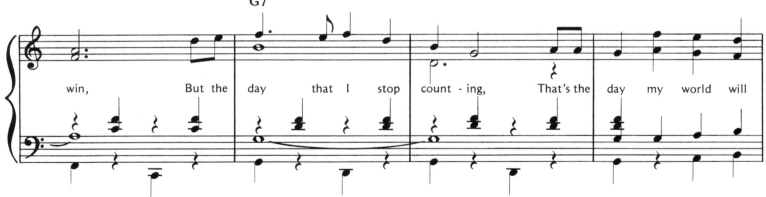

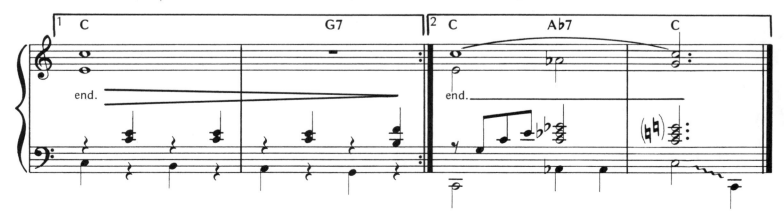

King of the Road

Electronic Organs
Upper: Flutes (or Tibias) 16', 4'
　　　　Add Percuss
Lower: Flutes 8', 4'
Pedal: String Bass
Vib./Trem.: On, Fast

Tonebar Organs
Upper: 80 8602 133
Lower: (00) 8601 001
Pedal: String Bass
Vib./Trem.: On, Fast

Words and Music by
Roger Miller

Automatic Rhythm: On

Moderately slow (with a beat)

Trail - er____ for
Third box____ car,

sale or rent:____
mid - night train:____

Rooms____ to let____ fif - ty cents;____
Des - ti - na - tion Ban - gor, Maine.

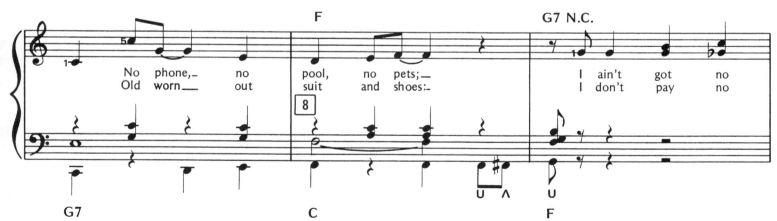

No phone,____ no
Old worn____ out

pool, no pets;____
suit and shoes:____

I ain't got no
I don't pay no

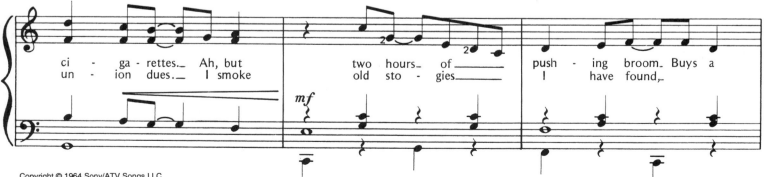

ci - ga - rettes.____ Ah, but
un - ion dues.____ I smoke

two hours____ of ____
old sto - gies____

push - ing broom. Buys a
I have found,____

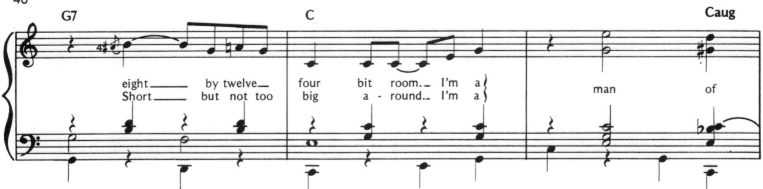

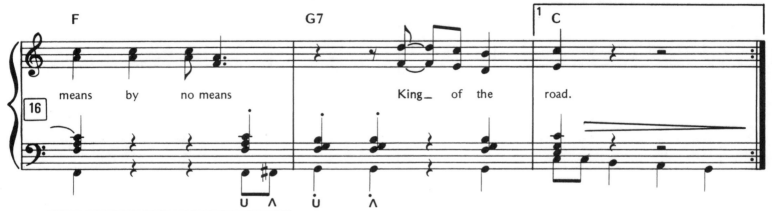

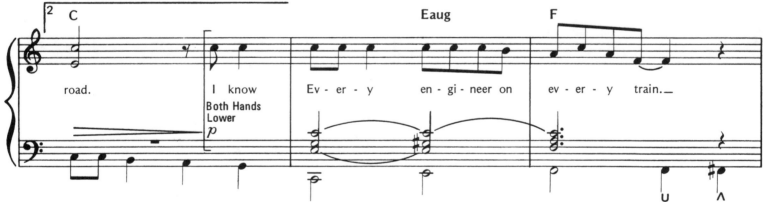

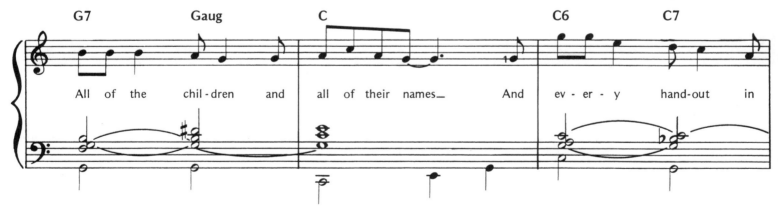

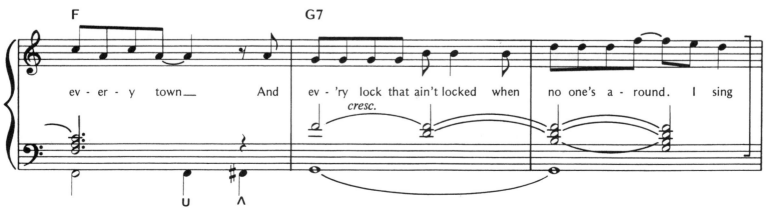

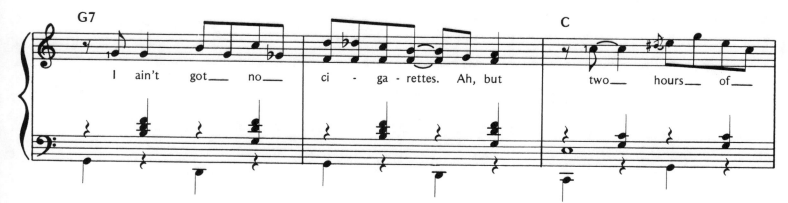

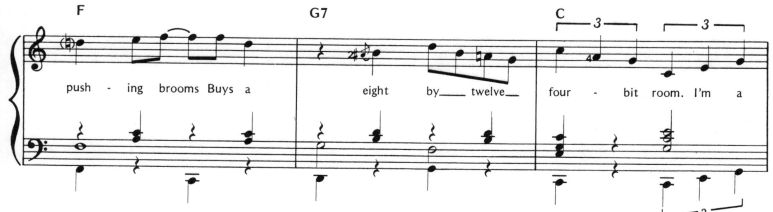

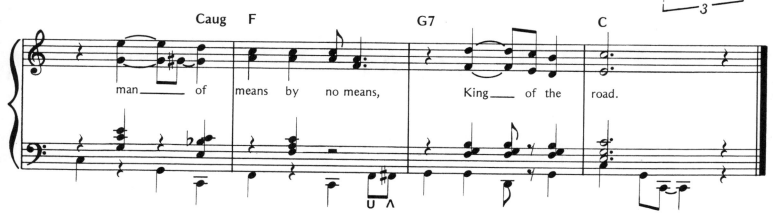

Heartbreaker

Electronic Organs
Upper: Flutes (or Tibias) 16', 8', 5⅓', 4'
　　　 Add Percuss
Lower: Flutes 8', 4'
Pedal: String Bass
Vib./Trem.: On, Slow

Tonebar Organs
Upper: 83 6030 400
　　　 Add Percuss
Lower: (00) 6402 003
Pedal: String Bass
Vib./Trem.: On, Slow

Words and Music by Carole Bayer Sager
and David Wolfert

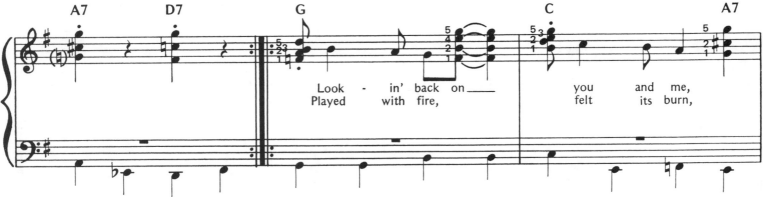

I Love

Electronic Organs
Upper: Preset Piano
Lower: Flutes 8', String 4'
Pedal: 16', 8'
Vib./Trem.: On, Fast

Tonebar Organs
Upper: Preset Piano or
76 5616 114
Lower: (00) 5325 112
Pedal: 35
Vib./Trem.: On, Fast

Words and Music by
Tom T. Hall

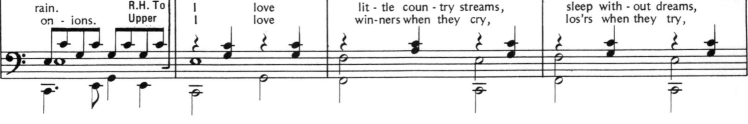

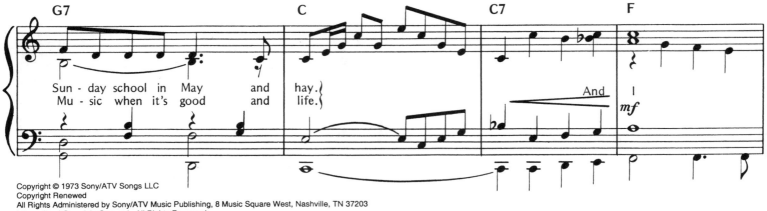

I'm a Fool to Care

Electronic Organs
Upper: Flutes (or Tibias) 8', 4'
         Clarinet
Lower: Melodia, Reed, Diapason
Pedal: String Bass
Vib./Trem.: On, Fast

Tonebar Organs
Upper: 40 8230 001
Lower: (00) 6402 000
Pedal: String Bass
Vib./Trem.: On, Fast

Words and Music by
Ted Daffan

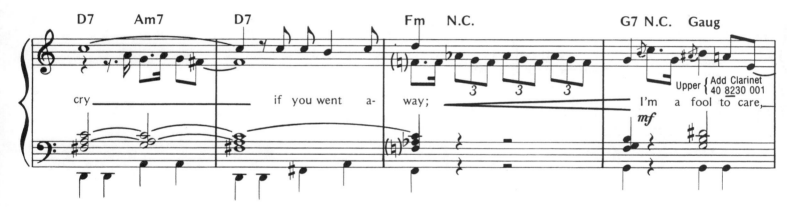

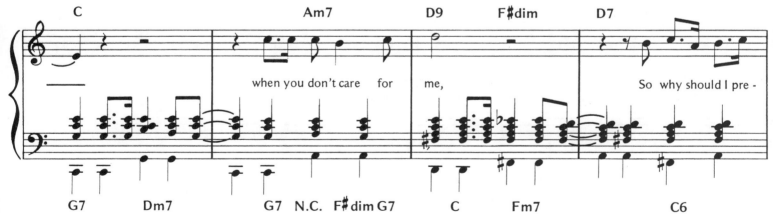

The Last Word in Lonesome Is Me

Electronic Organs
Upper: Strings 8', 4'
Lower: Flutes 8', 4'
Pedal: 16', 8'
Vib./Trem.: On, Fast

Tonebar Organs
Upper: 64 5613 000
Lower: (00) 8633 001
Pedal: 44
Vib./Trem.: On, Fast

Words and Music by
Roger Miller

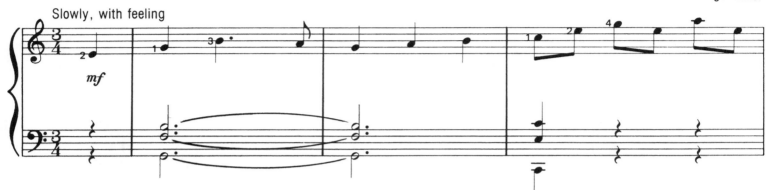

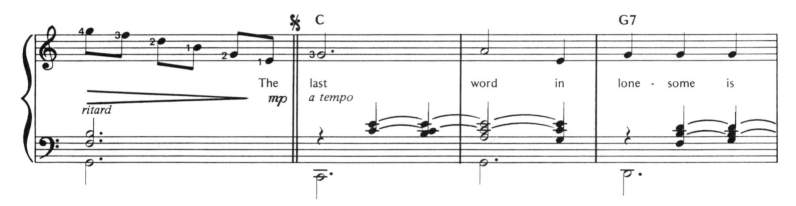

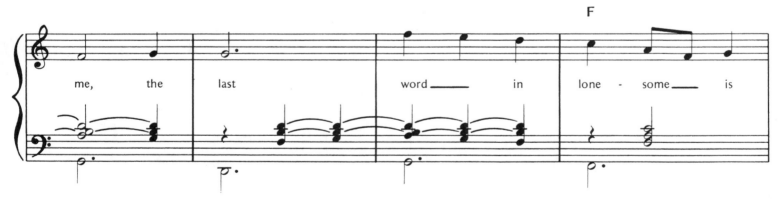

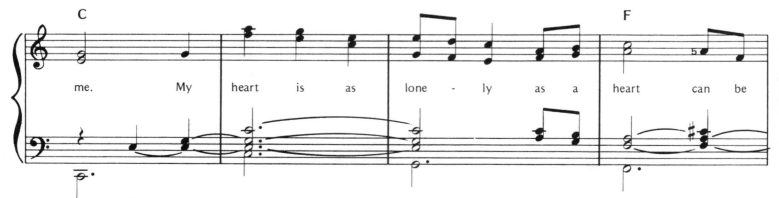

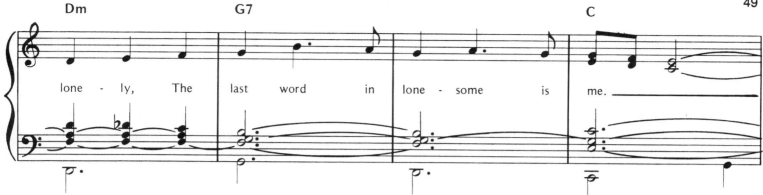

lone - ly, The last word in lone - some is me._____

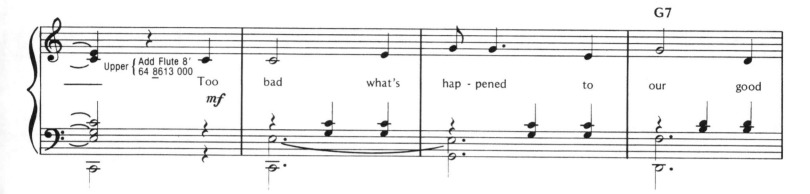

_____ Too bad what's hap - pened to our good

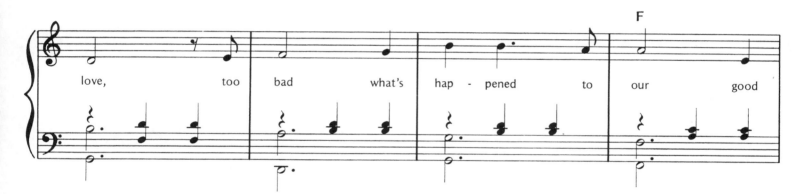

love, too bad what's hap - pened to our good

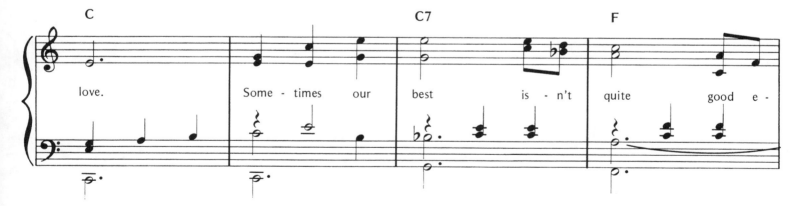

love. Some - times our best is - n't quite good e -

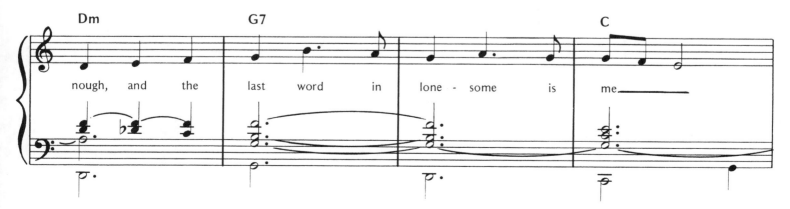

nough, and the last word in lone - some is me._____

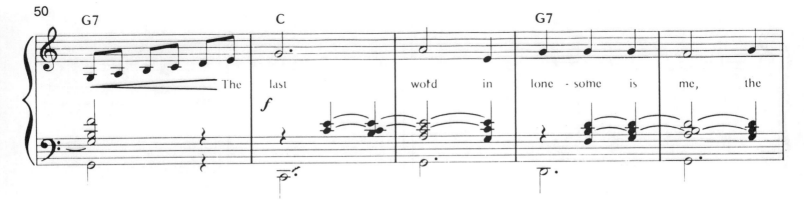

The last word in lone-some is me, the

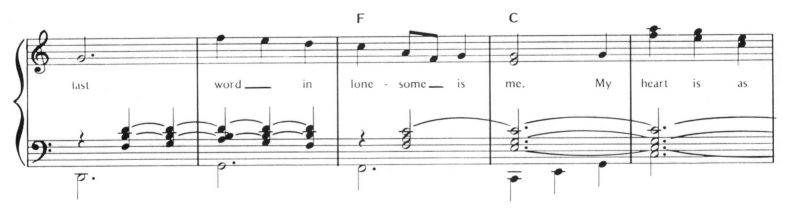

last word ____ in lone-some ____ is me. My heart is as

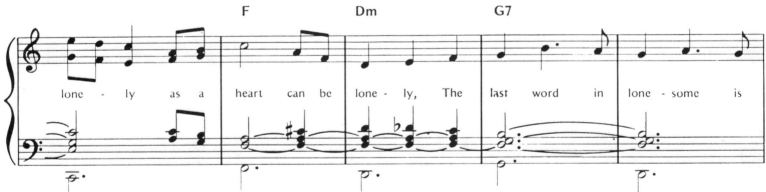

lone-ly as a heart can be lone-ly, The last word in lone-some is

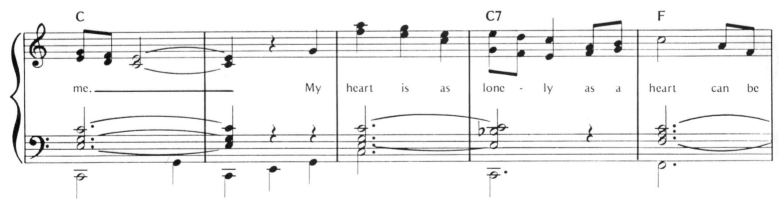

me. ____ My heart is as lone-ly as a heart can be

lone-ly, The last word in lone-some is me. ____

My Shoes Keep Walking Back to You

Electronic Organs
Upper: Clarinet 8'
Lower: Diapason 8'
Pedal: 16', 8'
Vib./Trem.: On, Slow

Tonebar Organs
Upper: 00 6270 400
Lower: (00) 4532 000
Pedal: 35
Vib./Trem.: On, Slow

Words and Music by Lee Ross
and Bob Wills

With expression

new
bye

And
And I

that's
can't

when I
for - get

miss
no

you
mat - ter

most
what

of
I

F   B♭   B♭m6   F   C7   F

all:
do:

R.H. to
Upper

And
my

arms

C7

keep reach - ing   for   you   My

F

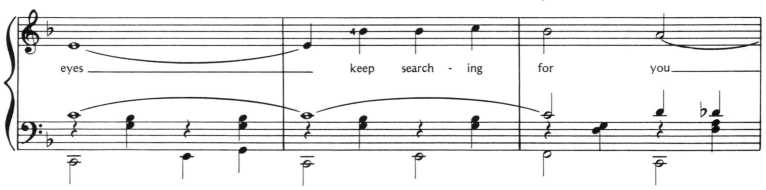

eyes   keep search - ing   for   you

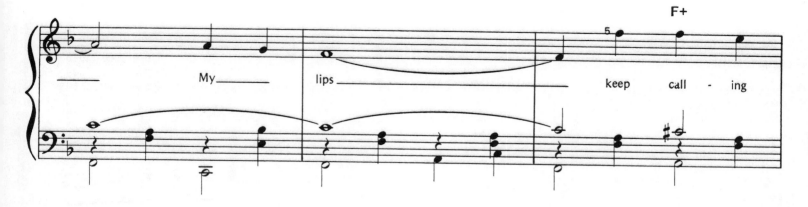

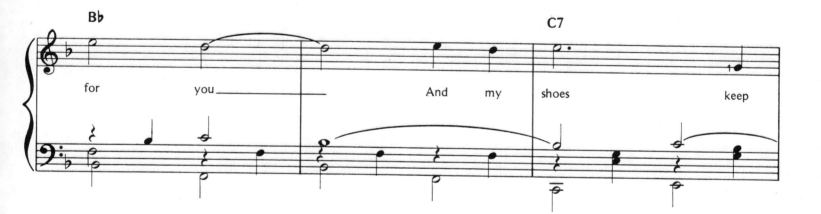

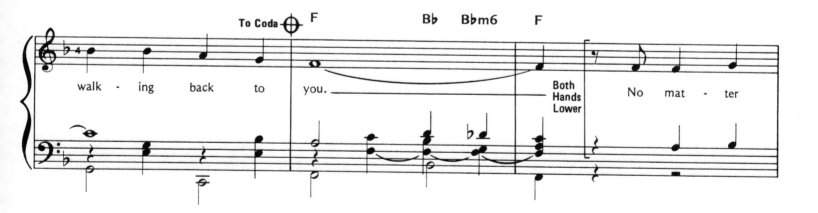

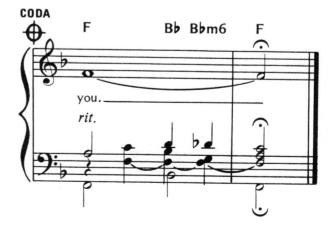

Make the World Go Away

Electronic Organs
Upper: Flutes (or Tibias) 16′, 4′
     String 8′
Lower: Flutes 8′, 4′, Melodia
Pedal: String Bass
Vib./Trem.: On, Fast

Tonebar Organs
Upper: 60 3616 111
Lower: (00) 7634 212
Pedal: String Bass
Vib./Trem.: On, Fast

Words and Music by
Hank Cochran

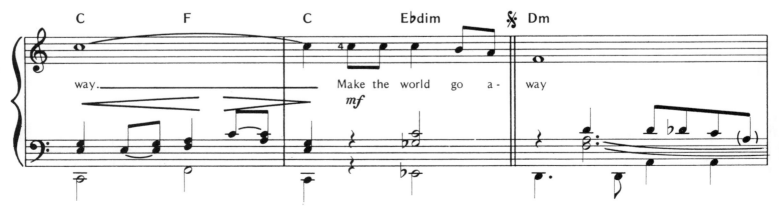

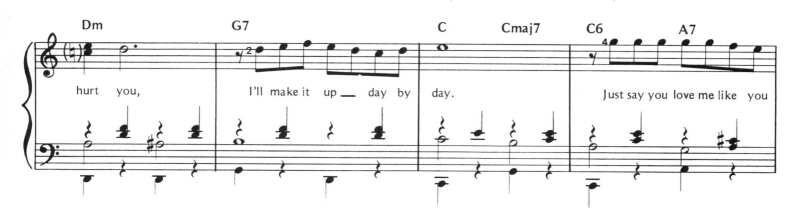

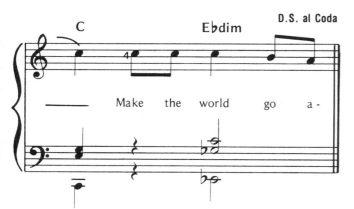

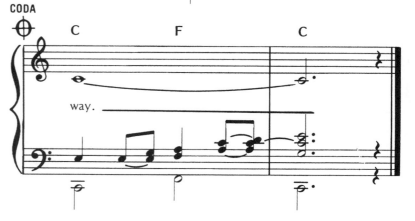

One Has My Name,
The Other Has My Heart

Electronic Organs
Upper: Flutes (or Tibias) 16', 8'
String 8'
Lower: Flute 8', Reed
Pedal: 16', 8'
Vib./Trem.: On, Fast

Tonebar Organs
Upper: 64 7434 000
Lower: (00) 8604 001
Pedal: 35
Vib./Trem.: On, Fast

Words and Music by Eddie Dean,
Dearest Dean and Hal Blair

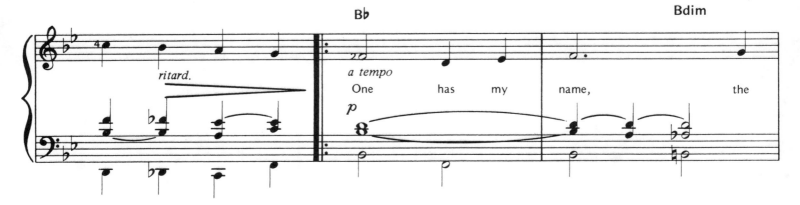

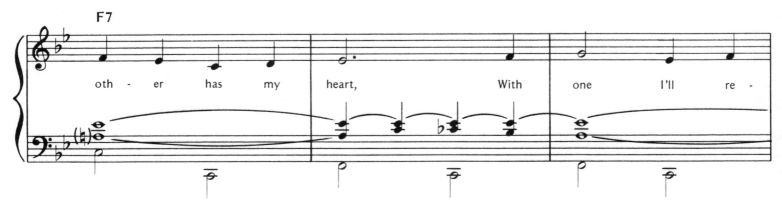

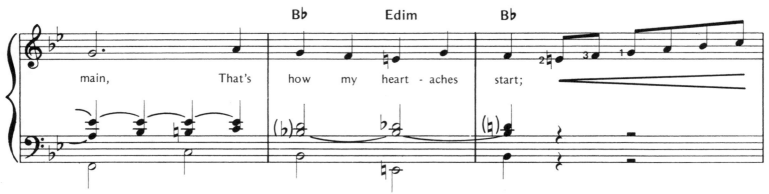

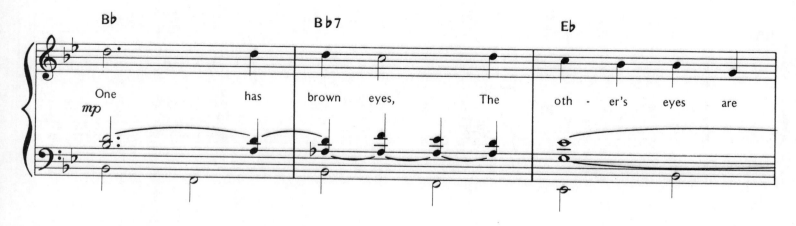

One has brown eyes, The oth - er's eyes are

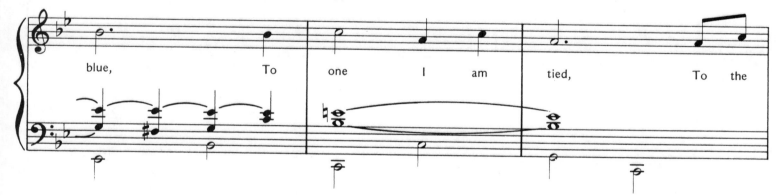

blue, To one I am tied, To the

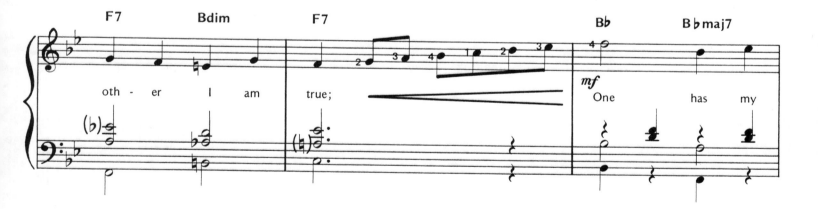

oth - er I am true; One has my

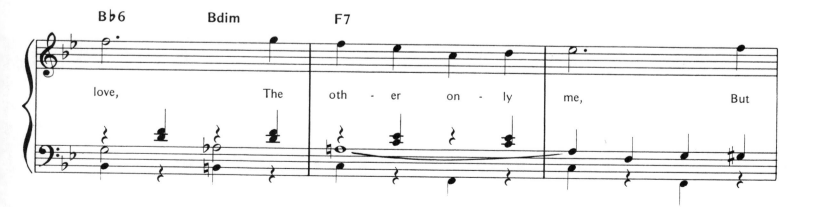

love, The oth - er on - ly me, But

58

Sail Away

Electronic Organs
Upper: Flutes (or Tibias) 16', 8', 2'
       Oboe
Lower: Flutes 8', 4'
Pedal: String Bass
Vib./Trem.: On, Fast

Tonebar Organs
Upper: 85 7023 000
Lower: (00) 8802 003
Pedal: String Bass
Vib./Trem.: On, Fast

Words and Music by
Rafe VanHoy

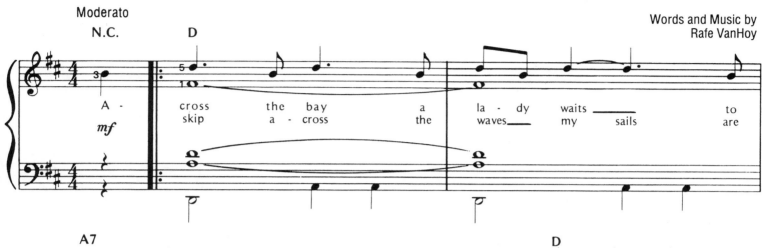

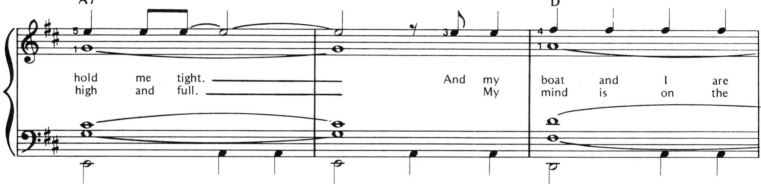

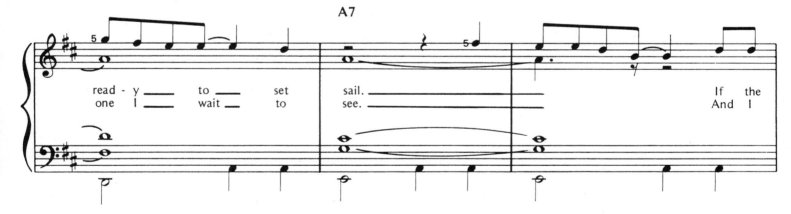

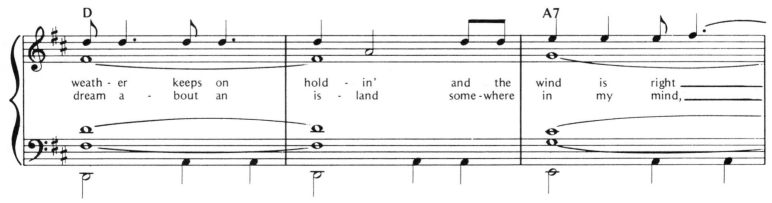

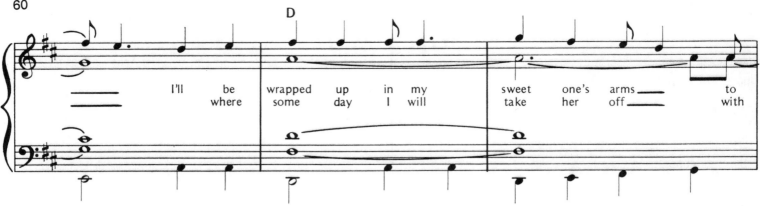

I'll be where ____ wrapped some up day in I my will sweet take one's her arms ____ off ____ to with

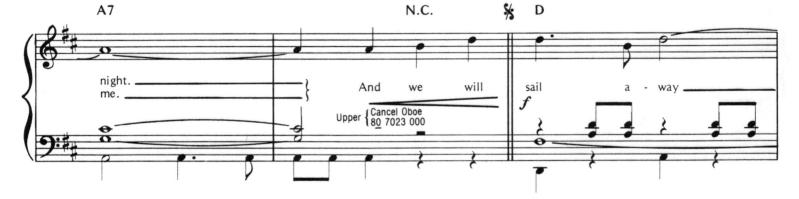

night. ____
me. ____

And we will sail a - way ____

Upper { Cancel Oboe
80 7023 000

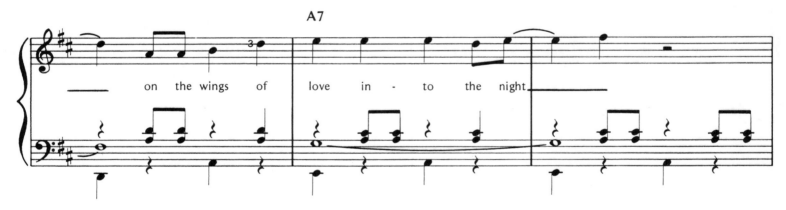

on the wings of love in - to the night ____

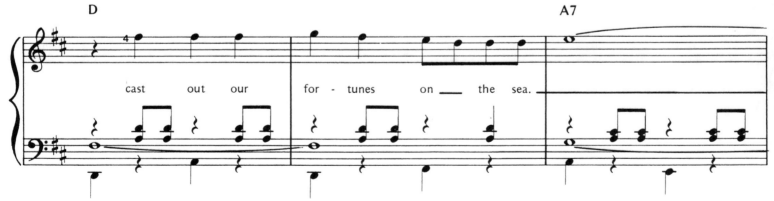

cast out our for - tunes on ____ the sea. ____

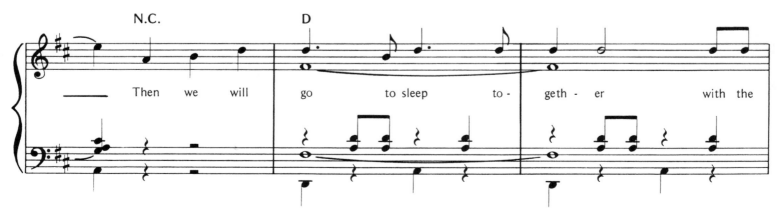

____ Then we will go to sleep to - geth - er with the

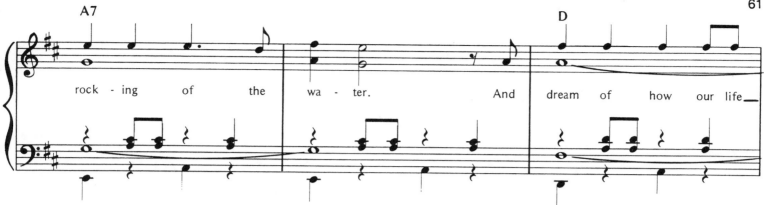

rock - ing of the wa - ter. And dream of how our life

will some - day be when she sails a - way with

me.

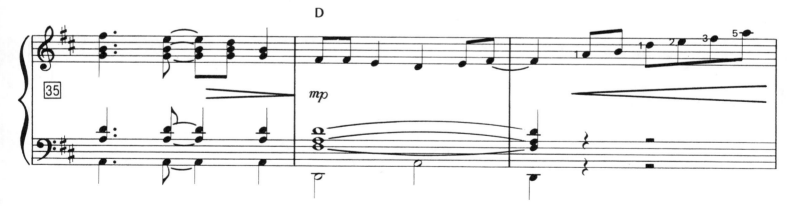

As I   And we will

Somebody's Knockin'

Electronic Organs
Upper: Flutes (or Tibias) 8', 4', 2'
　　　　Trombone
Lower: Flutes 8', 4', Reed 8'
Pedal: Bass Guitar
Vib./Trem.: On, Slow

Tonebar Organs
Upper: 82 5864 200
Lower: (00) 7103 001
Pedal: Bass Guitar
Vib./Trem.: On, Slow

Words and Music by Ed Penney
and Jerry Gillespie

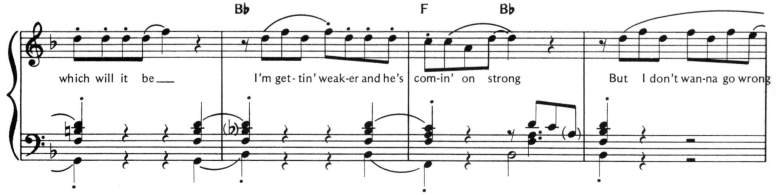

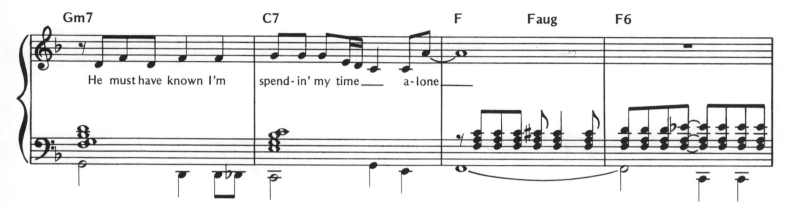

64

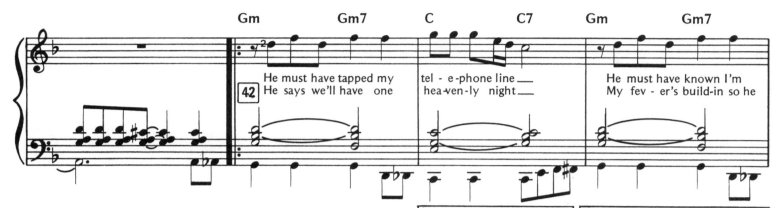

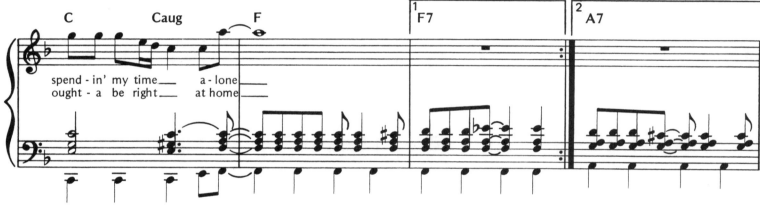

Walking in the Sunshine

Electronic Organs
Upper: Flutes (or Tibias) 16′, 4′
Lower: Flute 8′, Diapason 8′
Pedal: 8′
Vib./Trem.: On, Slow

Tonebar Organs
Upper: 80 0800 000
Lower: (00) 5303 000
Pedal: 24
Vib./Trem.: On, Slow

Words and Music by
Roger Miller

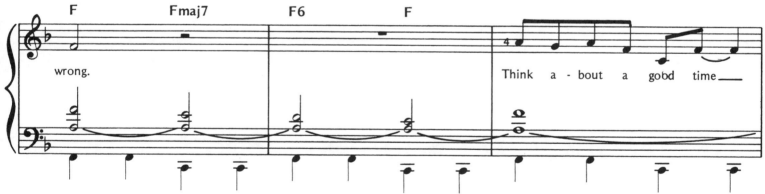

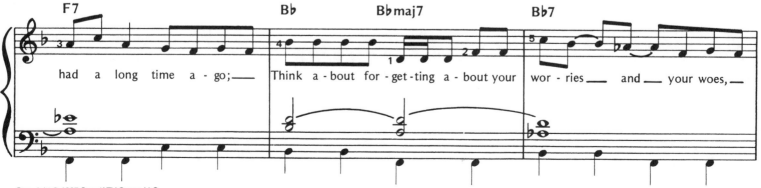

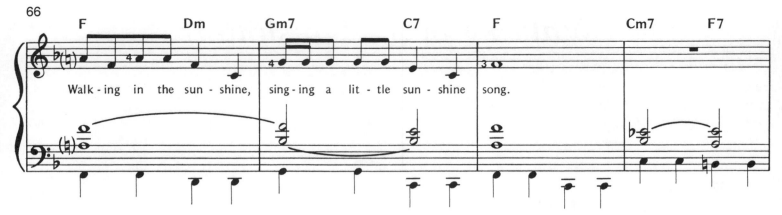

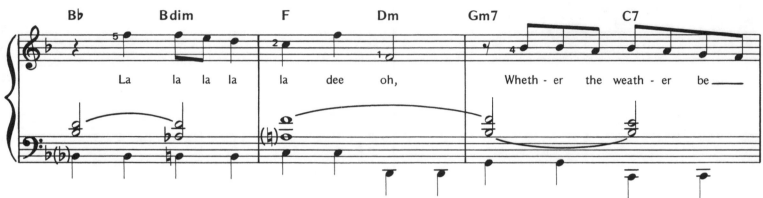

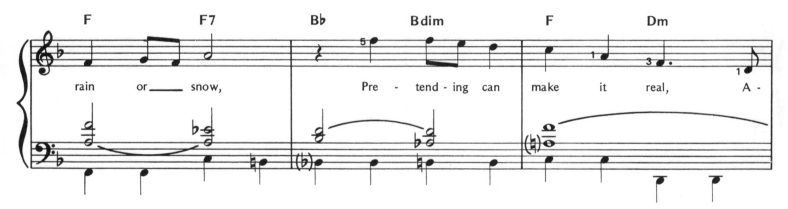

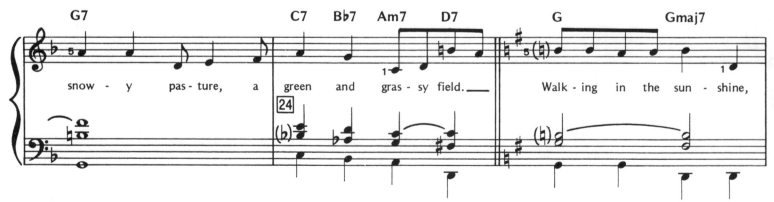

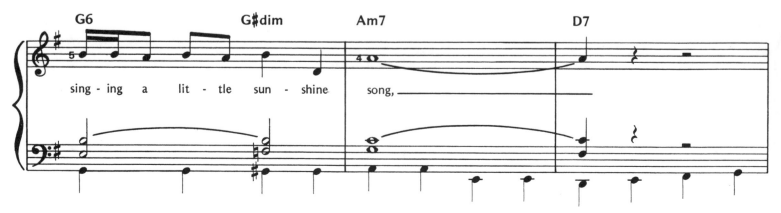

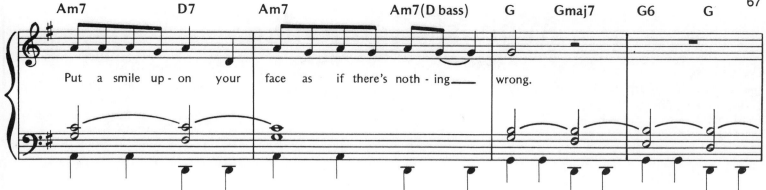

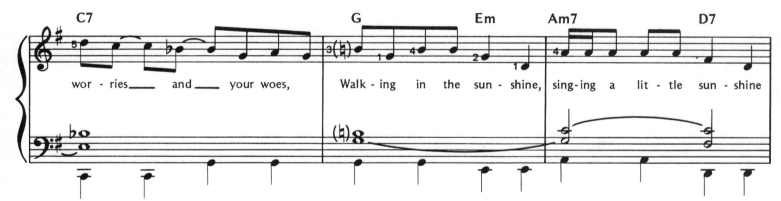

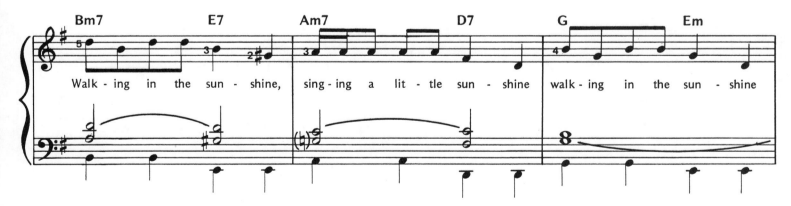

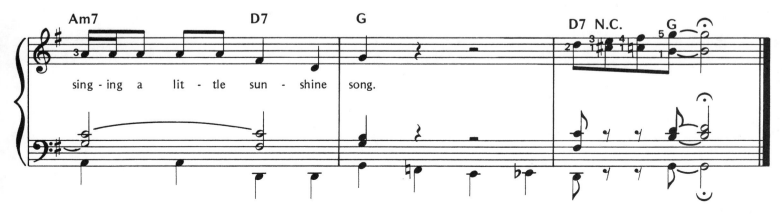

Wabash Cannonball

Electronic Organs
Upper: Flute (or Tibia) 8′
Lower: Flute 8′, String 4′
Pedal: Bass Guitar or String Bass
Vib./Trem.: On, Slow

Tonebar Organs
Upper: 04 8302 000
Lower: (00) 8504 001
Pedal: Bass Guitar or String Bass
Vib./Trem.: On, Slow

Words and Music by
A.P. Carter

With motion

From
out the wide Pa -
east - ern states are

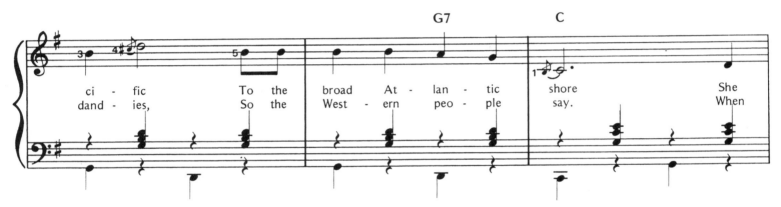

ci - fic,   To the   broad At - lan - tic   shore   say.   She
dand - ies,   So the   West - ern   peo - ple   When

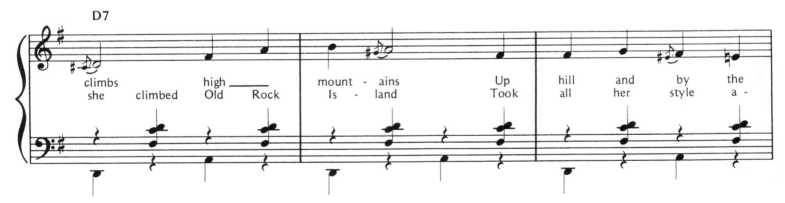

climbs   high   mount - ains   Up   hill   and   by   the
she   climbed   Old   Rock   Is - land   Took   all   her   style   a -

shore.   Al -   though   she's   tall   and   hand - some   And   she's
way.   To the   Lakes   of   Min - ne -   so - ta   Where   the

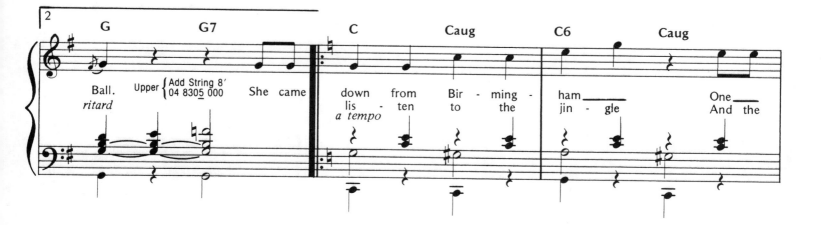

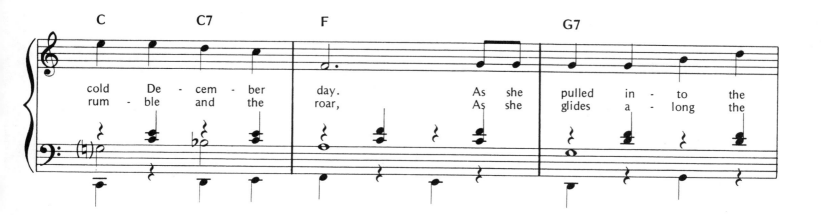

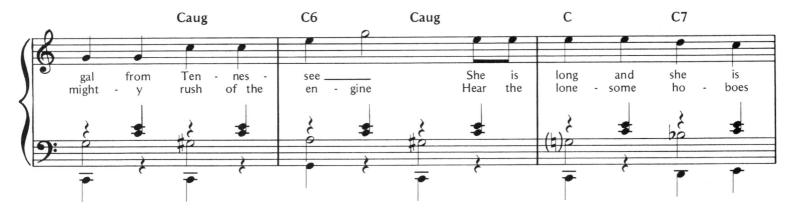

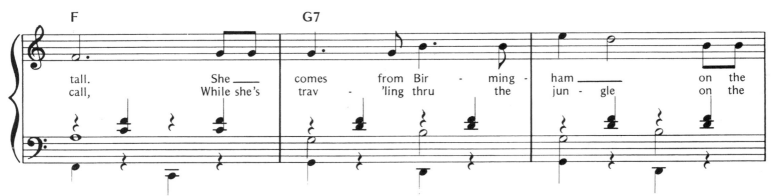

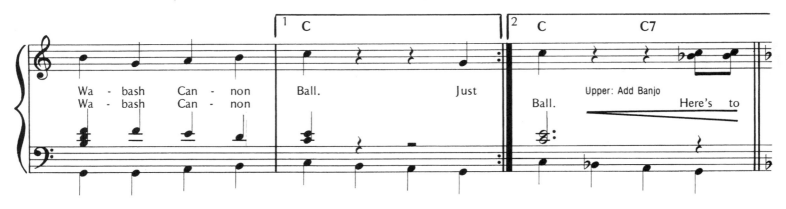

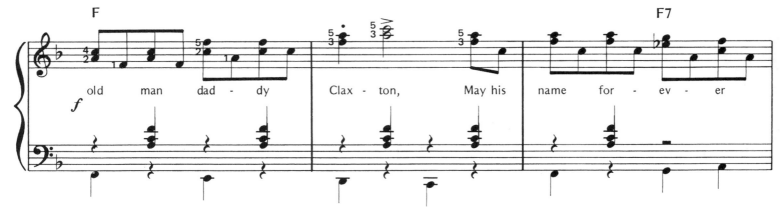

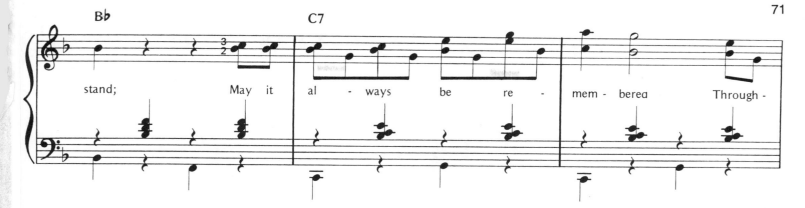

stand; May it al - ways be re - mem - bered Through-

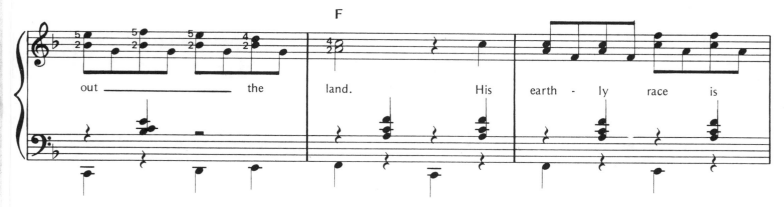

out _____ the land. His earth - ly race is

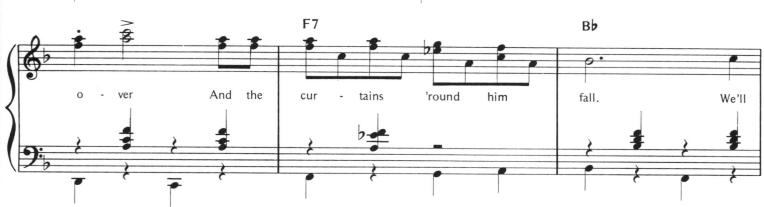

o - ver And the cur - tains 'round him fall. We'll

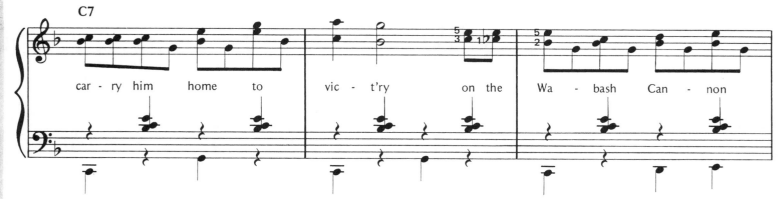

car - ry him home to vic - t'ry on the Wa - bash Can - non

Ball. _____

THE BEST SELECTION OF ORGAN MUSIC AVAILABLE

21 Contemporary Love & Wedding Songs

A collection of 21 contemporary romantic songs arranged for all organs. Includes: All I Ask Of You • Endless Love • Friends • Forever And Ever, Amen • Grow Old With Me • Just The Way You Are • So Amazing • Somewhere Out There • Too Much Heaven • Woman • The Velocity Of Love • You Are My Lady • You Needed Me • and more.
00290108 . . . . $8.95

50 Standards For Organ

50 favorite standards, including: Autumn Leaves • The Christmas Song • Hello, Dolly! • I Wanna Be Loved By You • A Good Man Is Hard To Find • Sentimental Journey • One • Unchained Melody • What I Did For Love • Witchcraft • and more.
00290291 . . . . $12.95

105 Favorite Hymns

105 songs arranged by Bill Irwin: Abide With Me • Amazing Grace • Ave Maria • The Church In The Wildwood • Holy, Holy, Holy • Just A Closer Walk With Thee • and more.
00212500 . . . . $10.95

Disney's Beauty And The Beast

Matching songbook to the Disney classic, including: Be Our Guest • Belle • Beauty And The Beast • Something There • and more.
00199109 . . . . $12.95

Irving Berlin Favorites For Organ

Arr. by Dan Rodowicz
23 Berlin favorites, including: Always • Blue Skies • Happy Holiday • I've Got My Love To Keep Me Warm • Puttin' On The Ritz • and many more.
00290251 . . . . $9.95

Christmas Favorites For Organ

24 great songs arranged for organ solo, including: I Heard The Bells On Christmas Day • I'll Be Home For Christmas • Rockin' Around The Christmas Tree • Rudolph The Red-Nosed Reindeer • and more.
00290249 . . . . $9.95

Contemporary Christian Classics

These 12 beloved songs have been arranged for performance on any organ. Music and lyrics are provided for such classics as: Behold The Lamb • El Shaddai • How Majestic Is Your Name • Upon This Rock • We Shall Behold Him • and many more.
00199100 . . . . $6.95

Country Standards For Organ

48 country favorites, including: Another Somebody Done Somebody Wrong Song • Crazy • Forever And Ever, Amen • Grandpa (Tell Me 'Bout The Good Old Days) • If We Make It Through December • Islands In The Stream • Make The World Go Away • Mammas Don't Let Your Babies Grow Up To Be Cowboys • Old Dogs, Children And Watermelon Wine • and many more.
00290228 . . . . $12.95

Easy Classics
arr. Jim Cliff
12 titles for easy organ: Chopin's Nocturne • Emperor Waltz • Jesu, Joy Of Man's Desiring • Ode To Joy (From The Ninth Symphony) • Vienna Life • others.
00276400 . . . . $5.95

Elvis!

40 songs arranged by Jean Tavens: All Shook Up • Don't Be Cruel • Hound Dog • Jail House Rock • Peace In The Valley • Return To Sender • Teddy Bear • Wooden Heart • more. Includes super collection of never-before-published color photos!
00212350 . . . . $12.95

Great Standards For Organ

50 timeless songs, arranged for organ, including: All At Once You Love Her • Call Me • The Entertainer • Goin' Out Of My Head • I Could Write A Book • I'll Be Around • If You Go Away • My Romance • Ol' Man River • Smoke Gets In Your Eyes • Under Paris Skies • Why Do I Love You? • Wonderful! Wonderful! • Younger Than Springtime.
00290207 . . . . $12.95

Latin Organ Favorites

Over 20 Latin favorites, including: Desafinado • The Girl From Ipanema • How Insensitive • More • One Note Samba • Quiet Nights Of Quiet Stars • and more.
00199107 . . . . $9.95

Les Miserables Selections For Organ

14 songs from this smash hit musical including: Bring Him Home • Castle On A Cloud • Do You Hear The People Sing? • I Dreamed A Dream • In My Life • On My Own • and more. Also includes color photos from the Broadway production.
00290270 . . . . $12.95

Disney's The Lion King

Includes all five songs from Disney's smash hit movie *The Lion King:* Be Prepared • Can You Feel The Love Tonight • Circle Of Life • Hakuna Matata • I Just Can't Wait To Be King.
00199110 . . . . $10.95

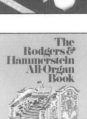

Phantom Of The Opera

9 of the best songs from the smash hit musical, including: All I Ask Of You • Think Of Me • Wishing You Were Somehow Here Again • and more.
00290300 . . . . $14.95

The Rodgers & Hammerstein All-Organ Book

Over 40 songs from hit Broadway shows, including: Oklahoma! • State Fair • Allegro • South Pacific • The King And I • Pipe Dream • Flower Drum Song • Cinderella • The Sound Of Music.
00312899 . . . . $12.95

Timeless Hits

33 favorites, including: Candle In The Wind • Could I Have This Dance • Forever and Ever Amen • I.O.U. • Just The Way You Are • On Golden Pond • Somewhere Out There • What A Wonderful World • and more.
00199105 . . . . $9.95